Number
Woman

Number
Woman

Hilary H. Carter

AXIS MUNDI
BOOKS

Winchester, UK
Washington, USA

First published by Axis Mundi Books, 2015
Axis Mundi Books is an imprint of John Hunt Publishing Ltd., Laurel House, Station Approach,
Alresford, Hants, SO24 9JH, UK
office1@jhpbooks.net
www.johnhuntpublishing.com
www.axismundi-books.com

For distributor details and how to order please visit the 'Ordering' section on our website.

ISBN: 978 1 78279 773 9
Library of Congress Control Number: 2014946458

A CIP catalogue record for this book is available from the British Library.

Design: Stuart Davies
www.stuartdaviesart.com

Printed and bound by CPI Group (UK) Ltd, Croydon, CR0 4YY

We operate a distinctive and ethical publishing philosophy in all
areas of our business, from our global network of authors to
production and worldwide distribution.

CONTENTS

Unity can only be manifested by the Binary. Unity itself
and the idea of Unity are already two.
Buddha

Introduction

All over the world people are experiencing a very strange phenomenon known as 'The 11:11 Phenomenon'. This is the mystifying appearance of the number 11:11 in their everyday life. It appears in a way that is so dramatic that there's no way it can be dismissed as coincidental. Nor can it be explained by attention bias because it happens to people who have never even heard of the 11:11 phenomenon.

There are also a significant number of people who are being bombarded with repeated digits, especially (but not restricted to) the numbers 222, 333 and 444.

I have experienced these unusual number phenomena. When the numbers first began to appear in my everyday life in the year 2003, their appearance was so dramatic and intense that I was frightened. I did a lot of research to try and discover the reason for this happening and to find the answer to the question, 'What does it mean?' However, none of the information that was available satisfied my curiosity. There were those who claimed that 11:11 indicated that portals were opening. I didn't under-stand what that meant and it didn't explain why I seemed to always look at the clock at 11:11 or why my shopping bill kept adding up to £11.11. Another school of thought was that 11:11 meant 'make a wish'. Well I guess that you could make a wish when you see it but that doesn't explain why you see it in the first place.

I was also noticing repeated digits such as 333 or 444. My research suggested that some people believe that these numbers were the angels speaking. If that was the case, then what were they trying to tell me and why did they use numbers rather than words?

What I really wanted (and what I couldn't find) were answers that explained why these strange number synchronicities appeared in my world and what messages (if any) they contained. I decided that whatever it took I was going to find the answers for myself. To do this, I would use the numbers as signs and follow them. That sounds like quite an easy and straight-forward thing to do. In 2003 when I began this bold experiment I could never have foreseen where this decision would lead.

My number journey has been at times difficult, challenging, uncomfortable and stressful. Yet it has also been exciting, inter-esting, illuminating, heart-warming and life changing. I have been totally transformed in the process in ways that have astounded me. For me personally, the gift of numbers has been the loosening of the hold of my ego. Can the path of number offer this gift to everyone who tries it? I cannot answer that because as far as I am aware, I am the first person on the planet who has walked this particular path.

I hope that my story will open your eyes to the world of numbers. Maybe one day you too will feel drawn to explore their messages. All that is required is courage, awareness, faith and the surrender of your ego.

Hilary Carter 2014
www.hilarycarter.com

Chapter 1

Hari and Bari

I lay down flat on my back on the bedroom floor and stared up at the dark wooden beams on the ceiling. I could hear the wind whipping through the crack in the single glazed window. The rising tide was lashing against the harbour wall and the masts of the yachts were clinking noisily. The storm was growing in intensity and the heavy rain thundered on the old slate roof. I breathed in the musty smell of damp that permeated the house. Another ceiling, another floor, another house. How many places had I lived in during the last decade? I worked out that I had moved house more than 10 times in 10 years. My lifestyle was not for the faint hearted, that's for sure.

The way that I live my life is unusual and quite possibly it's unique. That's because I use numbers to guide me on my path through life. Some people assume that I am mad to do that but I really don't mind what they think of me. I know that it takes courage to step out of the box of conditioning and to live an authentic life. It requires strength to walk my path but fortunately I have been blessed with a certain gritty determination to follow my truth regardless of what other people might think or say. I have always been brave. It has been running like a thread through my many lives on earth. I am the number woman and my role is to reveal the secrets of the world of numbers and number patterns to those that wish to hear.

Numbers began to make themselves known to me quite early on in my life. The first number to appear was the number 23, followed by the 11:11 time prompt. I searched for answers to explain why this was happening but I couldn't find any, at least no answers that made sense to me. That's when I decided to set out on my own personal quest for answers, offering up my

3

everyday life in practical research. As I progressed on my number journey, my intuition became finely tuned and I found the signs often led me to troubled places, in which I had a strong sense of a personal role.

I had just moved into the old house overlooking the harbour. It hadn't been an easy move. The house was somewhat neglected and run down and in my opinion it was barely habitable. However, on the path of number personal opinions don't count. Nor do likes and dislikes. All that counts are the number signs and they had guided me to the house overlooking the harbour so that's where I was.

However, the story I am about to tell you starts on the floor of a different house. Just one year earlier I had been lying staring up at a brand new ceiling because I had just moved into a partly built house in the English seaside resort of Torquay. I often spend time lying on my back observing my breath, just being in the moment and trying not to attach to any thoughts or feelings that might arise. I call it 'chilling' but these days that practice is called mindfulness. As I lay there gazing upwards a thought arose in my mind. It was the thought of my spiritual name, Hari. This name had been given to me by the late Yogi Bhajan, the yogi who brought kundalini yoga to the West. I tried to let the thought go but it persisted. Hari. What was the meaning of that name? I realised that I didn't actually know so I googled it on my phone and was very surprised when the following appeared:

'Bari is the capital city of the province of Bari and of the Apulia region, on the Adriatic Sea, in Italy'.

I had accidentally typed 'Bari' instead of 'Hari' as H and B are next to each other on the keypad. I corrected my 'mistake' and learned that Hari means 'he who unties the knot of material desire in the hearts of the living entities'.

About an hour later I was reading the newspaper and an advert for a tour of southern Italy leaped out of the page. It was flying directly to the Italian airport of Bari. I thought it was rather strange that Bari had made another appearance within an hour, especially as it is a fairly obscure city. When I looked at the price of flights to Bari, 9 out of 10 of them were priced at £111. Out of the 30 numbers on the website page there were 28 number 1s. Some people wouldn't have even noticed that. Others might have noticed but would not have attached any meaning to it. But to me, as number woman, I saw all those number 1s as a number repetition so I knew they were speaking to me. The line-up of 1s was so impressive that I took a photo of the screen and posted it on Facebook. Then I looked up Bari on Google maps to find out exactly whereabouts in southern Italy it was situated. As I did so I glanced down at the time in the corner of my computer screen. 11:02. The date was 21.01.2012. That is 21012012 @1102.

Most people wouldn't give those numbers a second thought but to me this was a number sign. 0, 1 and 2 in a neat little pattern is a clear example of number-talk so I knew I was being guided. The numbers were trying to get my attention and I was ready to listen to what they had to say.

As soon as my friend Kate saw my Facebook post she messaged me. She was impressed with the photo of the numbers. When I pointed out to her that she had messaged me at exactly 11:11 she was stunned. So was I. The 11:11 time prompt carries so much power that I rate it very highly as a number sign. All those 111s in conjunction with the date and time of this happening were too synchronistic to ignore. The numbers were appearing around Bari. I wasn't going to mess around or even think about it. I decided there and then that I would surrender to the number signs and commit to a trip to Italy. That's how the path of number works – instant surrender followed by action. If the number signs decide to guide me to Mexico or India or anywhere else in the world, I go. Even if it doesn't make any sense I go. The path of number cannot allow any interference from the mind. In fact the mind has to be kept out of the decision-making process altogether. Only intuition is involved in conjunction with the numbers as any actions needed to feel okay. I emailed Kate again to ask her whether she would like to join me in Italy. She acknowledged that she could see the signs but she needed to think about it first. Oh no. I could see what had happened. Like Alice falling down the rabbit hole, she had fallen straight into the mind trap.

"Don't *think*!" I wanted to shout because I knew that the thoughts of the mind were nearly always the block that prevented direct action. "Just *act*!" But I didn't interfere and I didn't say anything. Kate's life was Kate's life and the way she lived it was up to her. I am not in a position to tell anyone how to live his or her life. I would never do that. In this book I am simply describing how I use the language of numbers to guide me and you can make of it what you will.

Kate emailed me the following day with a photo of her cuckoo clock. It had stopped that very morning at 11:11. I was delighted because I could clearly see that it was yet another extremely strong number sign for Kate, confirming that she was needed in Italy. Yet still she felt that she couldn't commit. I was puzzled. The language of number synchronicity had spoken to her clearly and powerfully. I didn't know what else the numbers could possibly do to get her attention.

I had committed to the Italy trip as soon as I saw the signs. I didn't hesitate or question. I didn't consider the weather, my own personal comfort, the cost, the availability of accommodation or the details and endless possibilities of the itinerary and final destination. All those thoughts belong to the mind and the path of number is the path of no-mind. I need to stress this fact: mind interference is the block to action. I just took a leap of faith based on the appearance of the numbers and trusted that all would unfold perfectly. That's all. That's what I do. That's how I live my life. There had been enough number prompts to convince me that the trip was happening. End of story.

I had a strong feeling that Kate was part of the Italian journey because the number 2 was appearing along with the 1s and I know that Kate's favourite number is 22. She is also on a rare number 22 life path (see *Numerology Made Easy* by Hilary H Carter).

"Are you in or not?" I finally asked. "I need a decision from you. Whatever you decide is fine. I just need to know because I want to get there soon."

I knew I had to get to Italy as soon as possible. This made no sense. I was still involved in a building project in England, building a new house in order to raise enough money to continue my number journey. The house was almost finished and if I went to Italy I would not be around for the completion of the project. However, I recognised that although it didn't make sense to leave at this critical time, I trusted the signs and didn't buy into the fear or worry thought forms of the mind. I had lived as the number woman long enough to know that any actions I took based on number synchronicity always proved to be beneficial in the long run even though they almost invariably contained difficulties.

Following a spectacular display of even more number signs, all 1s and 2s, Kate decided she would join me. We were eventually guided to Lamezia Terme as our Italian destination, situated a few hours' drive south of Naples. I soon discovered that Lamezia was famous for 2 things: a very rare black crucifix and the statue of the dark-skinned Madonna of Romania. This was no coincidence. When I read about the crucifix I knew that I would eventually be led into a very dark place on this particular journey. I wasn't afraid. I have enough faith in the language of numbers to know that I will never be given more than I can handle. Nor would I be led into any situations that would harm me in any way. It was simply a case of surrendering to the signs and trusting the process. I was actually quite excited to see where the road ahead would lead me. One thing I can say with certainty is that my life as the number woman is very, very interesting. Since setting out on my quest for answers to the appearance of repeated digits and number patterns, I find myself living in a real life adventure filled with wonder and pure magic, as you will soon discover when you hear the rest of my story.

Chapter 2

333

The night that Kate made the decision to join me, she had a dream.

Kate: *In my dream last night I was clearly given 333 to watch for – it was very significant – scarily so. Ah yes – remembering now – page 333 in a very large book with a map on it – don't know what part of the world – I had opened a book and saw the page number was 333 and that the number was on the bottom of the right hand … Let's see what unfolds.*

Shortly after she had the dream, the number 333 began to appear to both of us. It was astounding. 333 was everywhere. I sent Kate an email at 3.33 (I hadn't intentionally chosen that time) and the next day I received one from her sent at 3.33.33. Even the seconds were taking part in this spectacular display of numbers. We each had to send 400 euros to pay for accommodation and the exchange rate in February 2012 meant that the apartment cost us exactly £333 each. Then the email confirming our booking was sent to us at 3.33.33. It was incredible, and way beyond our conscious control.

The agency requested payment with the date and time displayed as: 0220122320100000. They then confirmed receipt of the money in another email. Kate forwarded it to me with a note saying, 'Can you believe it?' Yes I could believe it. The confirmation email had been sent at exactly 11:11pm on 13.02.2012 (add them up…1+3+0+2+2+0+1+2). The 11:11 sign is a worldwide wake-up call on the spiritual path and it can take still my breath away. Somebody I know calls it 'a wink from God'. I like that.

I had taken a courageous step in deciding to follow the path of number. I had literally stepped off the edge of the known and into the unknown because I wanted to explore the 11:11 phenomenon and to discover whether numbers and number patterns had any meaning. It is true to say that I had lost a lot by choosing to undertake this experiment but I have gained so much more than I have lost. Sure, my life has changed beyond recognition and I now have nothing familiar to cling on to. In fact there is nothing in the outer world of form that I can attach to for security. The security that I once sought from the external world is now to be found within me.

The emails were flying back and forth between Kate and me. I was in middle of writing my book *No Name No Number, Exploring the 11:11 phenomenon*. This tells the story of my ownership of an ancient French convent that I had been led to buy by the number 11. The convent was the nearest thing to a home that I had. It was rather basic and not suitable for winter living. As part of my research for the book I was looking at the website of the healer Andrew Kemp. Andrew channels messages from other dimensions through the use of automatic writing. Once he had emailed me with a channelling that concerned that French convent. The channelling had proved to be stunningly accurate. He had initially introduced himself to me as a '33 man'. I remembered that well. I have a photographic memory when it comes to numbers. He emailed me to say,

Hi Hilary, I really enjoyed your '11:11' book. I'm a 33 man myself. I work as a therapist that may explain why it dominates my life. My treatment fee is £33. Andrew.

Andrew offers a free download of healing codes. I looked at the various numbers for the different forms of healing that were listed on his website. For example, the code for Divine protection is 954.258.347.777. But the one for Higher Self connection was 333.222 333.333. It's possible that this was a clue to show Kate and

I why the 222 and the 333 were appearing instead of just the usual 11:11. I forwarded the information to Kate.

Kate: Gulp…Higher Self connection… *It is why I want to go to Italy…nothing else…*

Kate, like many awakening souls on the planet right now, understands that we have a self with a small 's' and a Self with a capital 'S'. The small self is the ego, which is concerned with itself and all its wants, needs and desires. The Higher Self is our Divine Self. That's the part of us that is all wise, all knowing and all Love. Once we have surrendered our ego self to our Divine Self then we enter a new way of being. We begin to live for the good of all beings rather than for the good of the ego self. Giving up the ego sounds like quite a simple thing to do, but I was discovering that putting it into practice wasn't quite so easy. I was thankful that I had numbers to help, guide and support me as I travelled this path.

Chapter 3

Thomas Becket

By the time of the Italian journey I had been following number signs for years so I was quite at ease with spectacular synchronicities. Kate was gradually getting the hang of it and was opening up to the magic of being a number woman. She was reading a book called *The Way of Mastery* by Jayem, and just dipping in and out of it at random. One night she couldn't sleep so she read a few pages, put her bookmark in the book, closed it and then settled down to sleep. The next morning she brought the book downstairs to look up something and then she saw where the bookmark was...page 333. Not only that but the number 333 appeared at the bottom right of the page just like in her dream. The title on page 333 is FREEDOM IS LOVE UNDER ALL CONDITIONS. I asked her to send me a copy of the whole page as I thought it would be relevant. In the meantime, because of all the 333s appearing around the Italian trip, I knew that I needed to make contact with my 33 man, Andrew. I didn't really know what to say to him so I just sounded him out.

Hi Andrew, I am being inundated with the number 333 and I just know I need to contact you. It's phenomenal. It's everywhere. It only started once I decided to commit to a trip to Italy with a friend of mine. I don't know why I need to involve you and I'm not even going to try and guess. I'm simply following my intuition. The 333 is definitely linked to Italy and to you. So...what to say...should I just wait for you to respond and take it from there?
Love, Hilary

Hi Hilary, So, the big question, 333... I think it is about the power of 3s as triangles. I think each point represents a particular energy centre and if you make triangles out of 4 centres you end up with 4 triangles in a kite like shape. So the question for me is what are the 4 centres?

I have just moved into a Farmhouse, which – wait for it – sits upon the original site of a mediaeval Augustinian priory near Weston Super Mare. There is a new priory nearby but the original one – built by a knight racked with guilt for killing Thomas Becket – is on the land where we live and sleep. The energy is very strong.

I believe there is also a bigger picture and the location of all 4 sites sits within a larger grid, hopefully one you can unravel as you have done before.

If you do come back to England, it would be great if you could come and visit us here to see if you tune into anything. If things do unravel, we can tune in further and perhaps get some more precise detail...Best wishes, Andrew

Thomas Becket had been brought to my attention the year before when I had been researching really tall people as Becket was known to be an exceptionally tall man. He was the Archbishop of Canterbury in medieval England and had been murdered by 4 knights in Canterbury Cathedral. I had been to visit the site of his murder when I was staying with Kate because she lives in...Canterbury! Excitedly I picked up the phone to call her but then I saw that the time was 11.10. I wasn't sure whether to put the phone down and wait a minute because I normally pause at 11:11am every day to project a thought form of world peace. I'm not the only person who does this. Thousands of people all around the world pause for one minute and we all hold the same thought form. We understand that thought creates reality so the more people that hold this same thought form at the same time, the more powerful the effect. But then I decided that as I had already picked the phone up I needed to call at that time. Kate answered immediately. She was walking past the phone as it rang. I began telling her about the email from Andrew when I heard a man's voice interrupting.

"Just a moment," she said.

When she came back on I asked her who had interrupted her.

"It was my son. He's fixing my light."

"And what did he say to you? What were his very words?" I asked.

"He said, 'Where is the switch for the outside light.'"

"I think that might be relevant to us. He didn't say, 'Where is the light?' He said, 'Where is the SWITCH for the outside light.' Let's just register what he said."

"Okay. Do you think that it might be important?" she asked.

"Yes, I do," I replied.

"Why?"

"Because he said it at exactly 11:11."

Sometimes when a strong sign appears, the meaning of it isn't always clear. However, frequently it is followed by a second much clearer sign. Or it may be much later that the significance of the sign is revealed in which case I simply register the sign for future reference. That's what I did in this instance.

It was the night before the full moon in Leo and the Italian trip was all booked. It was my turn to have a dream.

I was in an old stone building, a rambling old property full of nooks and crannies. I was up on the top floor looking at the rotten wood and the leaking roof with a heavy heart. There was so much work to do. There were lots of people milling about. In the corner was a small child, no more than 2 years old, sitting on her mother's knee. She was holding a tablet about the size of an e-reader. She telepathically communicated with me, asking me to look at the tablet. There, in full colour, I saw all the lives I had lived. The past, present and future were all there on this small screen. This was amazing. I tried to tell her mother to look at what her child was showing me, but suddenly they both dematerialised in front of my eyes.

I couldn't interpret the dream but I wrote it down in my notebook as it was so unusual. Maybe the meaning of it would become clearer over the following weeks.

Chapter 4

Canterbury Cathedral

On 21.02.2012 (a rare palindromic date, reading the same backwards and forwards), Kate's photocopy of the 333rd page of the book *Way of Mastery* by Jayem arrived in the post.

LESSON 29: FREEDOM IS LOVE UNDER ALL CONDITIONS
Every time you hold an unloving thought you are going to experience the effect or the fruit of that thought. In reality there are two levels at which this occurs. The first is immediate. The second is mediated through the forms of time.

UNLOVING THOUGHTS ALTER THE CHEMICAL BALANCE OF YOUR BODY
In the first, in that which is immediate, the very moment you think an unloving thought as a physically embodied being, you immediately alter the chemical balance of the body and, thereby, experience tightness in the body, sadness perhaps, depression, an overall ill at ease feeling. For every negative thought, not just the big ones that you really get your attention wrapped around, but even the small ones, this is still true. Depression can only occur in a mind that has been denying its pathway to joy.

I knew I was being warned to watch my thoughts carefully. As we think, so we create. It was getting to the point where my manifestations were almost instantaneous. Just a day earlier I thought I had better go and leave a key with a neighbour in case I ever locked myself out of the house. I went out, shut the front door behind me and realised I had left the keys on the table so I was…locked out!

Every single email, text or phone call between Kate and I

continued to be accompanied by number signs. They were crazy. Mad. Mind blowing. We were on a journey like no other. We had moved way past anything that could be classed as normal. It was like being on a roller coaster, knowing that you had got on and you couldn't get on until the ride was over. All you could do was hang on tight and try and enjoy it.

On 22.02.2012 Kate emailed:

Well – I'm not sure what on earth is being prepared for us. Actually am not sure it is 'on earth' as I am having coincidental meetings BIG time about the 'other side of the veil'. As you know it's an area I would rather not open up to but the signs are coming thick and fast.

(Kate was a natural mystic but was fearful of developing her gift to its full potential.)

I feel moved to meditate on the knights who killed Becket. I was in the cathedral the other day with a friend…not a close friend, more of an acquaintance…and she said that she was descended from one of the knights who had killed Becket. I feel that I need to go to the cathedral where Becket was killed. I think I have to because that came in particularly strongly whilst writing this email to you…

I emailed straight back:

It's 14:44 on 22.2.2012. Look at the numbers on that email. It's clear that you must go.

Kate lived within walking distance of the cathedral. She decided to go and sit at the very spot where Becket had been murdered and I would tune in with her to see if anything happened. She texted me when she arrived at the main gate. I asked her whether she had texted me at 3:33pm on purpose but she assured me that she hadn't. Good, because any attempt to manipulate the numbers renders them powerless as signs. They only work as guidance if they arise unprompted and without any conscious mind interference at all.

We connected at 4pm. Kate was sitting in the cathedral and I was sitting on the floor of my half-built house in Devon, England. All we did was to sit in silence to see what would arise in our minds, knowing that our intention was to be in tune with each other at the same time. That evening we spoke on the phone to discuss our experiences.

"Before I left home – the words 'Original Source' danced before my eyes," said Kate. "There are Higher Beings who are seeking communication with us, evolved beings wanting the world to have the benefit of their wisdom through us – and it really is Higher wisdom. It's what is needed to come through for mankind. They are reaching down to us for connection and they will lead us with signs such as church bells."

"I thought it would be numbers rather than bells."

"Maybe it will be both. I got it really clearly that it was bells."

"So were you sitting at the very spot where Becket was murdered when you had these insights?" I asked.

"Yes I was. All the chairs in the cathedral had been put away so that visitors could sense how it would have been in medieval times. This time in history again seems like an important link for Italy. I went to the exact spot where Thomas Becket was slain. It was dark and rainy outside so there was fantastic atmosphere in the cathedral. As I sat there I connected to the legions of souls who had passed on from this life feeling enormous guilt and therefore expecting 'hell' after dying. In those times long ago it was clear cut. There was no grey area. When you died you either landed in heaven or hell according to how you had behaved during your one life on earth."

"I can't understand how anyone could swallow the theory of only living one life," I said, shaking my head.

"Times were different then, as you know. Anyway, this connection with all those souls was generated from looking at the red tipped swords of the knights who murdered him."

"What? The swords used in the murder were still there in the cathedral?" I asked incredulously.

"No, of course not. There is a modern sculpture on the wall. Hang on, I'll send you a picture."

The photo came straight through to my phone. It was accompanied by a title written in capital letters: GUILT. The sculpture hangs on the wall next to the spot where Becket had been killed. It is a modern sculpture of 4 swords that represent the 4 swords that had been used to kill Thomas Becket. It consisted of 3 swords and a broken sword.

When I asked why one was broken, Kate explained that it had broken during the murder.

"It was such a vicious attack. It happened as he was preparing for evening prayer. Someone came to tell Becket that some knights were arming and that he was in danger but he wouldn't leave. He seemed to know that his destiny was to be murdered in Canterbury. In fact he said as much to his congregation just before his death. Listen to this. It was written by Herbert of Bosham. He was Becket's biographer and he actually witnessed the murder.

'At the end of his sermon Becket predicted that the time of his departure drew near and that shortly he would be taken from them. And when he said this concerning his departure, tears rather than words burst from him.'"

"It's clear that he knew that he was going to die."

"Absolutely. Then I got the impression that our work is something to do with freeing those who are caught in guilt – well everyone is really – to free those in this life but also those in the so called next, those no longer in the physical. As you know, I have reluctance around working with disincarnate souls. Ah yes, we are talking about nothing less than original guilt. That is what is at the root of all guilt. Anyway, just before 4pm I spoke to one of the cathedral guides. He said the murder was particularly gruesome as the 4 knights who killed him had taken off the top of his head and one of them had scattered his brains on the floor of the cathedral. Also it was interesting that we tuned in at 4pm because it was 4pm evening prayers when he was slain. The guide said that following the murder, the knights went into exile, but I don't know where they went. I'm seeing my friend again on Saturday so I will ask her which knight her family was related to...and what happened after the murder...where they went etc..."

"Yes, and let me know what she says, please."

"Oh, and I got keys. Just an image of keys, that's it."

"Thanks for all that info, Kate. As you know I was in the new house in Torquay when we connected. I just sat and allowed any insights to happen. Most of the stuff coming through was very clear. I was told that Becket is responsible for the number 3 appearing and when we see it we are to know that it is him guiding us especially when it is repeated 3 times. He said, 'I am working with you.'

"Then I was given Rome and Sicily and that 3 people are involved in Italy. It could be you, me and Andrew or a third person we have not yet met. It's even possible that the third person could be Becket himself. I was then given an image of a skeleton to remind me of the tall skeletons that I had been researching when I was in Canterbury – the one and only time I have been there. Becket as you may know was very tall indeed. I was also given the square and the link was sacred geometry. Canterbury is part of the geometry and there is an island. I just kept getting 'island'. I also got 42 degrees. And Lucifer or Lucca, I'm not sure which.

"At exactly 15.55 my mobile went – I had forgotten to turn it off – and it was my daughter asking for my temporary address in Torquay. It's Ben Jonson Close. I was told there was a clue there and to look at the work of Ben Jonson. He's a playwright. He was a contemporary of Shakespeare. I'm not familiar with his work but I'll go to the library and take a look."

"But one of the books I'm currently reading is by Ben Jonson."

"It's strange that you should be reading one of his plays."

"No. It's not that Ben Jonson. It's a modern day Ben Jonson. He wrote a book called *The Healing Code*."

"That's an incredible synch. I clearly need to look at those codes..."

"Yes, do. You'll find them interesting."

So who was Thomas Becket and why was he suddenly appearing in my life? The first of those questions is the easiest to answer. He was the Archbishop of Canterbury in the 12th-century. This post was the most important position in the Church in medieval England. In those times the Church had great power over the lives of the people. The fear of going to Hell was very real and people were told that only the Catholic Church could save your soul so that you could go to Heaven. King Henry II wanted Becket to be Archbishop but Becket didn't want that and he said that their friendship would turn to hate if he agreed to the appointment. His letter would prove to be deeply prophetic. Eventually Becket yielded and took on the post of Archbishop. At that point he became a changed man. He threw himself wholeheartedly into his new role.

Then Henry and Becket fell out and Becket fled abroad for his own safety. It was 6 years before he felt safe enough to return to England. However, shortly after his return they argued again. Henry is said to have shouted, "Will no one rid me of this troublesome priest?" Four knights overheard what Henry said and interpreted his words literally. The knights were Reginald Fitzurse, William de Tracey, Hugh de Morville and Richard le Breton. On December 29th, 1170, they murdered Becket in Canterbury Cathedral. "For the name of Jesus and the protection of the church I am ready to embrace death," Becket uttered softly as he lay dying on the stone floor.

The site of Becket's murder became a shrine and a place of pilgrimage. Bits of his bones and drops of his blood were cherished as relics throughout Europe. Barely 3 years after his death he was canonized by Pope Alexander. The shrine remained until Henry VIII shut down the monasteries between 1536 and 1541. At this time all relics in Canterbury Cathedral were removed.

So that is a brief description of Becket's life and death but I had no idea why he was appearing in my life. I just couldn't understand why he would make his presence felt to me. It's not as if I am particularly religious or as if I have some strong interest in him. Surely a fleeting enquiry into his physical height the year before would not be enough to bring him into my sphere of awareness. I'd never thought about him, and until this episode, I had known very little about his life and death. No, I was genuinely puzzled and would just have to allow things to unfold in their own time.

Chapter 5

Lamezia Terme

We arrived at the Italian apartment late in the day, and that first night, as I lay in bed, I felt earth tremors. I mentioned them to Kate in the morning but she hadn't felt a thing. I knew what it meant. They knew I had arrived, 'they' being the forces of darkness.

When numbers guide me to places I often seem to land up at the scene of massacres or other gruesome events of centuries earlier. I believe that just by being on these sites, my physical body can be used as a channel for a down pouring of light that can help to penetrate and disperse the darkness.

"There's only one set of keys for the apartment," Kate informed me.

"That's not much good. We need a set each."

"I agree. We'll just have to get another set cut."

There was one for the gate, one for the main door and one for the apartment door. There was something deeply significant in the cutting of those 3 keys. The image of keys had appeared in Kate's meditations more than once and now keys were being linked with the number 3, Becket's number.

Our first day in Italy was a quiet day exploring the local area. Apart from a few original buildings and the harbour, the area around the apartment was remarkably ugly. In fact it was one of the ugliest places I have ever visited. Huge oil tanks blighted the view over the water. Unimaginative apartment blocks had been carelessly thrown up on any vacant plot. The beach was littered with rubbish, the walls covered in graffiti, there were weeds everywhere and there were even several burned out trains at the station. Thank goodness there was a railway station and a bus service so that we could get out of town.

A couple of days later it was the full moon in Virgo and we awoke to a brilliant blue sky. That meant that our planned trip to the cathedral in Lamezia Terme to see the black crucifix would be going ahead. We had wanted to go the day before but the rain had stopped us so we would be there right on the day of the full moon. The journey was difficult, and by the time we arrived black clouds hung threateningly in the sky above. There was no sign of any blue sky. Not only that, the cathedral was locked. We had travelled all that way and we couldn't get in. What's more, it wouldn't be opening its doors for another 6 hours. We couldn't understand it. We had travelled by train, waited 2 hours for a connecting bus and then walked a fair distance to reach the cathedral only to find it locked. We asked several people if there was any way we could find the key, but we were told it was not possible to open the cathedral until mass that evening. Those huge wooden doors remained firmly shut so we could not get to see the Black Crucifix or the dark skinned Madonna.

Standing there in silence under the shadow of the bell tower we both had the same feeling, a feeling of intense oppression. Kate kept getting the word 'strangulation'. Having asked for some answers to why the cathedral was locked and why we could not locate the key, I received a download. A download is like a message that comes from another part of me. I believe it is the Higher Self communicating with me.

It is not necessary for you to see the black crucifix. It is Hilary that so desires. The crucifix in question is not the root of the darkness. The root of darkness lies directly below your feet. It is deep in the bowels of the earth. You are standing on an axis of evil.

At that point I was given the image of what I can best describe as a massive black column penetrating deep into the ground.

We are using you as conduits of light to disperse and weaken the hold that the darkness has in this area. The channel in question links to the city of Naples and also to Palermo in Sicily. It is a long established channel and for that reason the hold is strong. Please spend time in silence so that we can use you to send down the light.

I told Kate what had been said and she decided to stand alongside me as the light was put through us. We knew that we were being used as transformers. We were standing beside a heavy metal railing under the shadow of the cathedral tower. After a while a shaft of light momentarily broke through the jet black sky and for no more than about 30 seconds we were bathed in brilliant sun. Then, just as suddenly as it appeared, it disappeared. But that was enough and we knew that this was a sign to tell us that we had done what was needed. As we left the heavens opened and water gushed down the street, cleansing the area where we had been standing.

Later that day I lay on my bed digesting the information I had been given. Then I had another download.

This part of Italy is held in a vice. The earth grid here is locked like nowhere else on earth. The source is below the Vatican in Rome. From there is a rope of darkness so strong and dense that it acts like a tether. The earth is struggling to break free and rise into a higher vibration. Your presence in the area is causing the tremors. It is the rope loosening. More shifting will come but we will protect you and keep you safe. You have felt the earth trembling below you. There is so much going on at the very densest level of existence. There are worlds below your feet that feed on fear. That is why the Mafia have such a stronghold here. They are able to operate in this area because of the lack of light. You are in the heart of darkness but you are protected.

It was only after my return to England some weeks later that I discovered that the Madonna and the crucifix were actually in Tropea cathedral, but we had been led to Lamezia Terme to stand on the place above an underground altar that was dedicated to the dark forces. I also worked out that Palermo was exactly the same distance from Lamezia Terme as Naples, thus forming a perfect triangle between the 3 places. Kate and I had therefore been standing on the precise mid-point that linked Palermo and Naples, two places that had strong links with the Mafia. When I have realisations like this I marvel at the intelligence of the numbers, how they can lead me to such an obscure place that aligns so perfectly with well-known places of darkness.

The Mafia were alive and well and the corruption in this part of Italy had wormed its way into society at a very deep level. Most of the people I broached the subject with simply refused to say anything. A young Russian student admitted to us that he had had dealings with the Mafia but he absolutely refused to be drawn any further on the subject.

"They're everywhere," he said. "And they're dangerous."

That is all he would say. It was the fearful expression in his eyes that spoke more than any words could ever speak.

In a small town that I will not name I met a man who showed me a deep, dry well under the cathedral, which was full of human skeletons. It had a glass lid and when he illuminated the well, I could clearly see all the bones. It was an eerie sensation to be looking at piles of human remains. I was struck with a flash of remembrance – the image of skeletons that Becket had given me.

"Oh, I see the Mafia have been here!" I joked.

"Yes, they are here. They are everywhere," replied the man.

"How do you know?" I asked. It seemed like such a regular kind of town.

"Everybody knows. A lot of people have dealings with them whether they like it or not. We all know who is Mafia and who isn't."

"And do they ever kill anyone?"

"Of course they do," he replied in a tone of voice that suggested I ought to have known that without asking. "I have seen people being killed. And they have no compassion. Man, woman or child. It's all the same to them. They're ruthless. Evil."

Then like a metal door closing with an echoing thud, he clammed up, realising that maybe he had said too much to this foreign stranger in a church. He had no idea who I was. I could have been a journalist...or a writer.

One day Kate and I took the local bus to the nearby town of Vibo Pizzo to check our emails in the internet cafe. It was a beautiful morning and we wandered around the lovely little town looking at the sights. There was a service taking place in the first church we visited. I poked my head around the door and was startled to see a mural of an eye in the triangle looking straight back at me, exactly the same as the one that appears on a dollar bill. I was aware that this symbol was linked to the Illuminati, a secret society that existed within a shadowy world, but I had never seen it inside a Catholic church.

The symbol of an eye had begun appearing in my everyday life several months earlier. I had first noticed it when I was putting my contact lens in. The single eye on my bottle of saline solution seemed to be staring at me. Then later that same day I was changing the bed sheets and I saw that each one had a label with the Egyptian eye on it because they were Egyptian cotton. In the evening I was stuck in traffic and I saw a huge single eye on the advertising board to my left. Searching for my bracelet that night I came across the one and only piece of gold jewellery that I own, a necklace with an amethyst set within an Egyptian eye. It had belonged to my Godmother who had died at the age of 60 from a heart attack. When I get a rush of signs one on top of the other like this I know that I am being guided to take note. I was being told that the symbol of the single eye was meaningful.

This was the first time I had seen the eye in a church and the church in question was a small, seemingly insignificant place. However, around the corner from this small church was a much larger one, San Giorgio's. I entered, noticing as I did so that there were 2 number 11s on the wall directly opposite the church door. Just to the side of the altar a young woman was kneeling at the feet of a dark skinned statue. She was deep in prayer and didn't look up when I entered. The statue had a dark brown face and was dressed all in black with a silver arrow pierced through a silver heart. A Black Madonna! I had no idea there was a Black Madonna in Pizzo so I hadn't gone looking for her. She had found me but I didn't know why.

Many months would pass before I would learn that she had been in my life for longer than I could ever have realised.

Chapter 6

Guilt

I looked for information about Becket and learned that he had been born on 21st December. That's the same date as the famous 2012 winter solstice and the date that the Mayan calendar ended. That, to me, was no coincidence. He was named Thomas because he was born on the feast day of St Thomas the Apostle. The very first holy image of Becket was created shortly after his death in Monreale Cathedral, in Sicily. Also, the principal church of the Sicilian city of Marsala is dedicated to St Thomas Becket. Kate and I had already planned to spend a few days away in 2 places: Sicily and Naples.

That evening I was sitting on my bed reading through my notebook when I came across the notes that I had written down after Kate and I had connected in meditation. They mentioned the 42 degrees. I wandered into the living room where Kate was sitting reading. She looked up as I entered the room and, noticing my serious expression, she asked me what was up.

"42 degrees," I replied. "I have just been reading my notes and I had been given 42 degrees. It was when you were in the cathedral at Canterbury and I was in the new house in Ben Jonson Close. You were given an image of keys and I was given 42 degrees. I'm just going to look at the map to see where the 42 degrees latitude runs."

I cleared the table, putting our 2 sets of 3 keys to one side then I unfolded the large map of Italy and laid it out.

"Oh no, I don't believe it…"

Kate looked at me quizzically.

"It's Rome. Rome is at 42 degrees north."

"I don't want to go to Rome." Kate said firmly. She sounded like I used to sound. Those words 'I' and 'want' are sticky ones.

They belong to the ego. Kate didn't want to travel all the way there, but then neither did I. Personal 'wants' and 'not wants' have to be put aside if you live in the way that I do. Following numbers requires surrender.

"Look!" she cried pointing to the television, which she had on in the background. "It says Rome."

By the time I turned round the word Rome had gone but the moment had been noted by both of us. We had planned to take one trip to Naples and one to Sicily. That was enough. Adding Rome to the agenda would be an awful lot to cram into a 4 week visit.

"Look at the clock," I said.

"21.21."

"21.21," I repeated. "That's 2, 1, 2, 1." I sighed. "It's a number pattern. We are being spoken to."

We looked into each other's eyes. She knew. I knew too. The language of number was telling us that we were needed in Rome.

"This month is really important. This year is important. It's 2012. I know we don't want to go to Rome, but you had already emailed me telling me that there are Higher Beings who are seeking communication with us. Now they're obviously communicating with us and we need to listen."

"Bari!" shouted Kate, not answering my question. For some unknown reason Bari was now written at the bottom of the television screen. It was of course Bari that had originally guided us to Italy.

"I'd much rather go to Bari. I've never been there and I enjoy going to new places."

"Kate, we might have to go to both by the look of it..." I replied, looking more closely at the map to remind myself exactly how far we were from Bari. I moved the map and both sets of keys fell to the ceramic floor with a loud crash. Keys, keys...the keys were speaking to me. Maybe there was a key to Becket in Rome.

I continued reading my notes. I read them aloud to remind Kate what had been said. When I reached the following sentence I almost shouted it.

"I was given Rome and Sicily," I read. "Rome. Oh, I'd forgotten that…"

"So had I," replied Kate.

"You sent me that photo too. I still don't understand why you put 'guilt' in the subject box," I said.

"Because that's what it's all about for me. If we could all just for one moment remember our innocence. When you delve deep into your – and I'm talking about anybody's mind here – original guilt is at the root of all guilt."

I didn't really understand what she meant. Original guilt sounded a bit deep to me…

"Mind you, I bet those knights felt guilty when they realised what they'd done. They killed Becket because they thought the king wanted him killed, but he didn't."

"Yes, I know. I wish I could remember where they went after they had killed Becket."

"I'll have a look on the internet," I said. That's when I found out that they had fled to Rome. The Pope was a friend of King Henry II so they went and they were protected by the Pope. It was now 100 per cent clear that whether we liked it or not, Rome was on the agenda.

"But I'm not going into the Sistine chapel," insisted Kate. "I've been to Rome before and even then I refused to go in because it felt so evil."

"I'll go in if I need to. I'm not afraid. Well that's not really true. It would be more accurate to say that I'm not afraid of being afraid."

So, our pilgrimage had taken an interesting turn. Kate and I would now be heading for Rome via Naples. One of the confirmation signs following our decision to go to Rome was when we discovered Henry II's year of birth: 1133, a rather neat combination of 2 very significant numbers. Confirmation signs are great. They appear after a decision has been made as if to confirm that decision. I always say a silent thank you when they appear. I'm not sure what would happen if they didn't appear because I have never had to face that situation.

That night, once again, I was woken by the bed shaking. The earth was gently rumbling underneath where I slept. It clearly felt as if something deep in the bowels of the earth was making its presence felt and warning me not to interfere with the status quo. I was not afraid. Nor was I going to be stopped.

I'm a lightworker who is being guided by numbers and I'll do the work that I was put on earth to do.

Chapter 7

Healing Codes

Bari had appeared twice, once with the £111 flights and again on the television following the appearance of Rome. Intuitively I knew that it had been shown to me as a location on the grid that linked in to Rome. It formed a triangle between Naples and Rome. The grid in this area was revealing itself bit by bit. A visit to Bari was not necessary. Awareness of its link in the sacred geometry was all that I needed. That's why it had been brought to our attention. The work that I do involves the physical body. I knew that by being in Naples and Rome the light force that would be shining through me would affect the blocks in the etheric grid of the earth at a deep enough level to clear the block in Bari.

Neither of us wanted to go to Rome. Kate had been there quite recently and had seen all she wanted to see if looking through the eyes of a tourist. I had not been for years but I knew that I needed to go, not as a tourist but as a light worker. The Vatican was calling. I knew that when I went I would be standing in the very heart of darkness. I wasn't exactly looking forward to being in the eye of the storm but I would do it. I would be used as a conduit. A huge force would be put through me. The concentration of light needed to be at its highest possible power to penetrate into the density of darkness that I knew had its source below the earth at this point. This work was not being done by our limited ego-selves but by our Higher Selves, also known as our limitless Divine Selves. So we both yielded to the signs and booked our tickets to Rome.

The night before the trip to Rome I woke at 4am. The bedroom was freezing cold. It was the slimy type of cold that indicates the presence of dark or earthbound entities. I have seen what this slime looks like. Some years ago my ex-husband and I bought a large detached house that had previously been the local undertakers. In the garden was a double storey outbuilding that used to house the chapel of rest and the coffin-maker's workshop.

"I don't want to live there. It'll be such an unhappy house," I said.

I knew that it was a house of sorrow. Most of the people walking up the path to visit the place over the decades would have been visiting the dead bodies of their loved ones. I didn't want to live in a house of grief, but my husband didn't see what I saw. He just saw a large studio space suitable for housing his equally large paintings.

"But look at the size of the workshop. It'll make a fantastic studio."

My husband was an artist and his priorities were different to mine.

"You can rent a studio. Let's find a proper home to live in."

He wouldn't be dissuaded. In the end I agreed to move in on the condition that if the house was too spooky and uncomfortable for me then we would sell it and move on. We duly moved into our new home on a Monday morning. The next night my husband left to take care of business in London, leaving me alone in the house with our baby daughter. In the night I woke up to a slimy coldness. Despite the fact it was July, the room was freezing. I sat bolt upright and there, hovering at the end of my bed in mid-air, was a greyish green sludge. I was frightened and I recited every prayer of protection I knew and gradually the gunge dissipated and the temperature in the room returned to normal. Now I was experiencing exactly the same thing in Italy. This time I wasn't afraid. I knew I was protected. Darkness couldn't harm me. I chanted my mantra and fell back to sleep. Then I had a dream.

I had to go into church to clear it by chanting the sacred mantra 'Om'. I was omming, loudly and intensely so that the vibration of that sacred mantra would fill every corner. Someone sent the police to stop me. When they arrived I pretended to be devout catholic by praying. Then they arrested me. I met the force of darkness in the guise of a man in a trilby hat. He was so evil. I tried telling myself that darkness didn't exist so not to fear it, but I felt the force of it. Then I said to myself that light always overcomes dark, but I could feel that the power of the darkness and I knew that this man in the trilby hat tortured people through mutilation of the genitalia, both male and female.

Then I woke up. As I lay digesting this dream, something was happening to the top of my head. I felt as if someone or something was hitting it with a soft book or a cloth, a strange sensation at my crown chakra, the highest of the 7 chakras that link directly to the physical body. Maybe I was being prepared for the visit to Rome.

The train to Rome left at 9:33am. I sat in seat 33. I was given seat 33 on the way back too, even though I had not selected it when booking the ticket. I was glad of those confirmation signs. I picked up an Italian magazine that someone had left lying on the seat next to me. It fell open at a picture of a single eye. I smiled to myself.

The train sped along the track reaching speeds of over 220mph. That is how it is when you are on track. It's possible to make very rapid progress. The delays occur when we come off track, as I know from personal experience. As we hurtled towards Rome I felt as though I was an actress playing a part in a film. I had felt this way before. It was a feeling of detachment from what I was experiencing, like being an observer of my life. I almost felt as though I could pause, play, fast forward or rewind my life just like in a film.

If I was in a film and I wanted to pause it, I would press the pause button. Look at the pause button. It is exactly the same as the number 11. If I press it again it restarts the movie, so the 11:11 is neither stopped nor started, it's between stop and start. I believe the 11:11 sign shows how to get to that place where there is no movement, where there is no go or stop. The way out of the movie that the mind is constantly creating is to be between stop and start, the end of one section before the beginning of the next, in that place of stillness, the place of perfect balance. Some might call this zero point.

The train journey to Rome wasn't a pleasant experience because the woman sitting next to me was really annoying. For the entire journey she kept pressing the buttons on her mobile phone. Each time she pressed the button on her phone it was accompanied by a very loud bleep. I guess she was a bit deaf and had put the volume up to maximum. I'm fairly patient but after more than an hour of loud bleeping it really began to get to me.

"I wish she'd bloody shut up," I said to Kate, nodding my head in the woman's direction. "That bleeping is getting on my nerves."

"Rather than connecting into it you could say, 'Thank you, I forgive you, what can I learn, what is my lesson?'" replied Kate.

"Lesson?" I asked.

"Yes. She's obviously pressing an ego button of yours. Instead of being resistant to it, which causes a block or a barrier, move into it. There is something there to be healed. This is what Ben Jonson talks about in *The Healing Code*. You find whereabouts in your body the feeling occurs and then take yourself back in time to when you first felt that and heal it from that initial trigger. The bleeping affected you because you hooked into it and it prompted something within you that needs healing. You responded with annoyance. I hardly even noticed it."

"I can't believe that."

"It's true, but that girl with her headphones on so loud got to me, that relentless thudding of her music."

Although I had noticed it, the headphone noise hadn't affected me in the same way as the bleeping.

"So I hooked into the bleeping and wasn't bothered by the

headphone noise and you hooked into the headphone noise and the bleeping didn't bother you."

"That's true, yes. Probably most other people were not affected by it because they are not carrying that pattern. They didn't have that particular button. Everything around you in your everyday world has been created in love to allow you to heal and get free, so you need to look at why the bleeping affected you so much."

"Maybe it has something to do with the fact that I could never find silence as a child. At the age of 2 I already had 3 siblings. I never had my own room, not until I left home at 18. I always had to share my space with my sisters and I constantly longed for space and silence."

"How can you be quiet when it's noisy around you?"

"I don't understand what you mean. Surely it's not possible."

"Well, if you don't tune into it a noise you won't really hear it. There were other noises going on like the thudding headphones, but you didn't key into that."

I tried not tuning into the beeping, but it was no use. It just kept on pressing my button.

"Are you saying once you have no ego absolutely nothing ever will bother or disturb you?"

"I'm saying that your world is what you choose to tune into, or not."

These words struck me as important. They had come to me via Kate and through Ben Jonson. Both Kate and the name Ben Jonson had personal links to me so I knew I should take note.

Chapter 8

The Day of Blood

We arrived in Rome on March 15th, the Ides of March, forever linked with the murder of Julius Caesar. If it hadn't been for a Facebook contact called Angela, the fact that it was the Ides would probably have passed me by. I had never met Angela. We had begun corresponding after she read my book *The 11:11 Code*. Angela was being given number signs and she got into the habit of running her signs past me. I read her numerous emails and responded to them. In return Angela helped me a lot for she saw things that I didn't see and she pointed things out that I had missed. Virtually every one of her emails was sent at a significant time or contained something that had meaning for me.

In ancient Rome, the Ides marked the beginning of a 10-day rite in honour of Attis. And what a strange and disturbing rite this was. There are several versions of this myth but they all have 2 main things in common; Cybele's great love for Attis, and his act of self-castration.

Attis was a handsome young shepherd who was loved by the Goddess Cybele, the Great Mother of All Things. Attis fell in love with someone else and Cybele became insanely jealous. As revenge, she drove Attis into a fit of madness. He ran wildly through the forest and castrated himself under a pine tree. There he bled to death. From the ground that absorbed his blood the first violets sprung up, which is why these flowers are associated with Attis.

Once a year a pine tree was wrapped in a linen shroud, decorated with violets and placed in a sepulchre in the temple. This represented Attis. On the Day of Blood or Black Friday, the priests of the cult cut and mutilated themselves with knives so they bled. There would be blood on the altar and their clothes were soaked in blood. It was a really bloody ritual. They danced ecstatically and some of the more pious male devotees of Cybele castrated themselves, holding up their bloody organs to the heavens to make themselves eligible for the priesthood. This reminded of my dream about the man in the trilby hat who mutilated genitalia.

Two days later, a priest opened the sepulchre at dawn, revealing that it was empty and announcing that Attis had been resurrected by Cybele. On discovering that Attis has been resurrected, a wild and joyful celebration takes place. This is known as either 'Hilaria' or the 'Day of Joy'.

I was stunned when I found out the name of this festival and you will understand why when I explain the reason. The 'H' in Hilary H. Carter refers to my spiritual name, Hari. However, the name given to me at birth was Hilary Joy Carter. Hilary Joy. That's very similar to Hilaria Joy. I had been given 2 names that linked me directly to the Ides of March and the festival of Attis. I believe that is because I had been destined to be used for the work in Rome.

It was Angela who brought another odd synchronicity to my attention. She informed me that March 15th (The Ides of March) was normally written as 3.15. Do you know what the 315th day of the year is? It's November 11, or 11.11 (except in a leap year).

It is said that the initiates of this strange cult of Cybele worshipped a black stone. There is a black stone at Mecca too. In the eastern corner of the Grand Mosque is an ancient stone building called the Kaaba. Wherever they are in the world, at certain times of the day Muslims point their bodies in the direction of Mecca. According to Muslim tradition, this mysterious stone dates back to the time of Adam and Eve. I have seen pictures of it. It is broken into pieces, set in a silver mount (silver is the metal linked to the moon) and draped with a veil. It looks extremely feminine in nature. Could the stone of Cybele and the Kaaba stone be linked? Could they even be the same stone? And where does the Black Madonna link in? Is she an extension of the original cult of the feminine energy that began with the worship of the black stone? My journey was becoming complex, deep and challenging but I wasn't going to give up. I would continue, regardless of whether those answers would be revealed to me or not, for on the path of number one cannot have attachments, not even an attachment to expectation.

Chapter 9

The Vatican

Kate and I were being supported and helped every inch of the way on our pilgrimage to Rome. We didn't need to do anything. Everything was simply delivered to us. We pulled into Rome railway station, and as we did so, the first thing I saw was a billboard with the word PAUSE written in huge letters, complete with a large picture of the pause button and its distinctive number 11. We had not booked a hotel and we were short of time because we wanted to get to the Vatican before sunset. However, seconds after getting off the train we were approached by an official tourist information guide. We told him our budget for accommodation and he took us to a hotel right next to the station. He showed us where to buy the bus ticket and where to catch the bus to the Vatican, so we quickly dumped our backpacks in the hotel and set off. On the bus on the way to the Vatican an American girl overheard us talking about our destination and told us exactly where to get off.

The number 33 appeared on several occasions on the bus journey, once on a man's jumper and again on a billboard. That was a double 33. There was a digital advertisement screen blasting out its unwanted advertising to the captive audience of bus passengers. Suddenly the all-seeing eye appeared, advertising a 3D cinema experience. It was appearing more and more frequently in my life. I still didn't know why. I was aware that we were on our way to the 'Holy See' which could be shorthand for the symbol of the all-seeing eye.

Less than an hour after setting foot in Rome we had arrived at the Vatican. We were not regular tourists. We were there to do a job. I didn't know what the job was, other than it had to do with penetrating the field of darkness that was well established at that site. However, as I approached St Peter's square I immediately knew exactly what was needed. Directly in front of the Basilica was a huge obelisk.

"I have to be in contact with the obelisk. I need to lean against it and act as a channel for the Divine Feminine energy," I said to Kate.

"I think I'll stand in front of the Basilica. What do you think?"

"Yes, that's fine. Whatever feels right to you is perfect." I totally trusted Kate's powerful instinctual nature. I'm sure she had no idea that she would be standing beside Cybele's temple because the Vatican supposedly stands on the exact location of the original temple. These days Christians celebrate the death and resurrection of Jesus Christ on the same place where the death and resurrection of Attis had once been celebrated. They even decorate their homes with pine trees at Christmas, a strong link to the Attis myth.

I climbed over the metal railing surrounding the obelisk. Nobody stopped me. It was a warm sunny day and the sky was blue and cloudless despite the fact that it was the middle of March. The sun was shining on the western side of the obelisk, casting a dark shadow to the east. I needed to face east so I stood in the shade of the obelisk. The moment I leaned back against it, the bells tolled 3 times. It was half past 3. A double 3: 3:30pm. Perfect timing. And it meant we would be there when the clock reached 3.33pm. I knew I didn't need to do anything in particular as I leaned there with the base of my spine against the obelisk. Simply being there and allowing myself to be used as a conduit would enable an energetic balance to take place. This work needed 2 of us as it was magnetic in nature. There I stood on the Ides of March against the undeniably masculine obelisk with the Divine Feminine energy flowing through me.

I began to rock even though I was leaning against the obelisk. My lower back leaned against the hard, cold stone. The lower back is the location of the sacral chakra, part of the human energy system known about by yogis. There was so much guilt around sex in the Catholic religion, so much oppression and control. Light poured through me to begin to dissolve this guilt. Several times I was sharply jolted. I was standing in the shade of the obelisk and Kate was on the steps of the Basilica in the full light of the sun. Light and dark. It felt very symbolic. We stood until the bells tolled 4 times, indicating quarter to 4. Kate had mentioned bells being used as signs and it was happening. As the bells tolled I began circling the obelisk in both directions. I was given the image of a band of light about fifty centimetres wide that was woven with a geometric design. I wound this geometric light firmly to this pillar of darkness. Again I stood. When I looked for Kate I saw she had moved. She was in front of a large statue of Saint Peter who was holding a huge key and pointing his finger. Momentarily I remembered how she had been given the symbol of the key in Canterbury Cathedral. I had no idea if Saint Peter was relevant to the unfolding events or not. My eyes met Kate's eyes and together we walked off in the direction of the Vatican gates.

"Are you going into the Sistine Chapel?" asked Kate.

I shook my head.

"Not necessary," I replied. "But the city needs light."

"Rome?"

"No, Vatican City. It's a city in its own right you know. A city within a city."

We walked past the gates, past the huddle of nuns standing on the steps, past the Vatican guards in their uniforms and carried on around the corner. There was a huge wall all the way around the Vatican, carefully monitored by security cameras, but nothing could protect the place from warriors of light. I knew I had to take the etheric light webbing that had been wrapped around the obelisk all the way around, thereby circling the entire city with a geometric web of light. That was the first time I had ever used light in this way. Normally it is a thread of light that over time grows into a river, in the same way that a small trickle of water can grow into a stream and then a river. It can't normally be seen by the naked eye. All I do is visualise the light as I know that energy follows thought. Sometimes the etheric world broke through into the physical world and at those times I did see the light. Sometimes it was silver or gold. Other times it was coloured.

We started walking. I chanted a mantra of protection and love as I walked. Kate followed behind me. I was keeping as close to the huge sloping wall as possible. It was a bit hair-raising at times because there was not always a pavement to walk on. Turning blind corners on roads in Rome is a dangerous occupation, but I knew I would be kept safe. It was quite a long walk and Kate soon began to get tired.

"Don't you think that's far enough?" she asked.

"No, I have to go right round. I have to surround the city with a mesh of light. It needs to be tethered to the obelisk."

We continued walking. After another 10 minutes or so Kate stopped.

"It could be miles," she said. "How far is it?"

"I've no idea. I don't think it will be that much further. We're just doing a circle so we're bound to eventually come back to where we started. I'll know when we're finished. Either I'll be given a sign or I'll just get a knowing."

Kate sighed and on we walked, the speeding cars narrowly missing us on several occasions. We must have looked strange, 2 women walking on the busy road in the opposite direction to the traffic. In some parts there was a pavement and then the going was easy. At that time I didn't know that the Vatican only covered an area of about 0.44 square kilometres. It is the world's smallest state, with a population of less than 1000, none of whom are permanent residents.

"Here feels much lighter," said Kate as we arrived at a grassy part with trees. I glanced up and saw a CCTV camera pointing in our direction.

"No, it's not here. We haven't finished yet. We need to go all the way round and back to the obelisk."

"I'm too tired. I don't want to go any further. It could be 5 miles or even longer. The Vatican is a city so we're walking around a city. I want to turn back."

"If you want to turn back that's okay with me, but I can't turn back. I am here for a purpose. Tired or not, I must finish the work. I could walk right round and then come back and get you."

Kate hesitated. She could be waiting for hours for my return. I had no idea how long it would take me to complete the circuit.

"I know. I'll ask that man with a dog the direction to St Peter's square and if he points back to the direction we have come from then we'll know it's a really long way, but if he directs us in the same direction we're walking, then we're over half way round."

We were in luck. We were sent in the direction we were walking so we continued onwards. Allowing for stops, it took over an hour to walk the circuit, surrounding that dark site with chanting and light. Returning to our hotel as the sun was setting, I was shattered in a way that I have never experienced before. I felt as if I had been hit over the head with a hammer. As soon as my head touched the pillow I was out for the count, falling into a long, deep and dreamless sleep.

Chapter 10

The Obelisk

The days after the Vatican light webbing were not easy. I felt okay the next day on the 6 hour train journey back to the apartment. It was in the evening that I began to feel that all was not well. I was aware that I had stirred something up and attempts were being made to infiltrate my energy field. I guess it was inevitable. One cannot walk into that level of darkness and expect the status quo to remain. Imagine how thick a rope has to be to tether a ship. Now imagine how thick it has to be to tether part of the earth. That's how thick the rope of darkness was. I cleared my aura with incense and set up protection in my bedroom. I had experienced a black magician (Satanist) attempting to infiltrate me once before, just before the publication of my first book. I was not afraid because I knew that I had the tools and techniques that would keep me safe.

That night I slept with my raw sapphire around my neck. I had bought this incredible crystal from a man in India several years earlier. It came from Nepal. I had been walking along the street outside the Sai Baba Ashram in India when a Nepalese man came running up to me.

"I have a crystal for you," he called out to me as he proceeded to physically drag me into his shop. I was curious so I allowed him to show it to me. He produced a rather ugly piece of bluish rock from below the counter. It was the size and shape of my little finger, a strange slightly rusty looking stone glued to a silver mount so that it could be used as a necklace.

"That?" I asked in slight disgust. "That's not a crystal"

"It is. It's a raw sapphire."

"No it's not. Sapphires are blue and shiny," I replied.

"This one is raw. It hasn't been polished. It's very special and very, very old. I know it is meant for you."

He placed it in the palm of my hand and that was it. He didn't have to say another word. I knew it was mine. I didn't even haggle on the price. I simply paid him what he asked and left the shop with this amazing object.

The crystal had been charged and cleansed it in the ceremonial Havan fire at the Babaji Ashram in England so now it was a powerful form of protection. Despite that, I woke at 4am, choking. It was as if someone had me by the throat and I was gasping for breath. As I woke I just caught the tail end of a dream. In the dream I was in a shop paying for something and the till receipt ended in 1111 as did my credit card.

Kate was not well. She had started feeling ill on the way back from the Vatican clearing. She was getting hot and cold and she felt weak. I knew how unwell she was when she said that she wanted to stay indoors and rest. Normally she can't sit still. I'm not surprised that we had been affected by Rome after I discovered something about the history of that cold stone obelisk I had been leaning against. Not only was it absolutely ancient, but it was one hell (appropriate word) of an obelisk that had seen more than its fair share of death, darkness and suffering. It had originally been erected near the Egyptian pyramids. It had presided over Nero's countless brutal games and Christian executions. This obelisk had witnessed centuries of brutality and murder, including games where Christian children were dressed as sheep and torn to pieces by wild animals for the entertainment of the Romans. It is one of 13 obelisks in modern day Rome, a city with more obelisks than any other city in the world. Below the obelisk is a line that marks the winter and summer solstice. Although it is 82 feet high, it used to be twice that height.

I had already been to the obelisk in Central Park, New York when I had visited the Ground Zero site several years earlier. That obelisk and the one on the Embankment in London are a pair.

At the time of our planetary healing work in Rome, Pope Benedict XVI was the Pope. According to Saint Malachy he is the 111th Pope. Saint Malachy was a 12th-century Irish monk, who, while on a visit to Rome in 1139 had a vision. The vision was a list of the next 112 popes that would rule from that time until the End Times. He wrote short descriptions in Latin as to how each Pope would be identified. Somehow his written vision was lost in the Vatican for 400 years. When the documents were rediscovered in 1595, remarkable similarities between the prophecy and the popes over the previous years were noted. Saint Malachy also predicted the place and time of his own death: Clairvaux, France, on All Souls Day, November 2nd, of that same year. That is the day after All Saint's Day, November 1st (1.11). He did indeed die on that day.

Chapter 11

Sicily

The black crucifix was symbolic of the darkness that had infiltrated the southern part of Italy. The darkness ran deep into the earth, deeper than any tunnel system. We were in Mafia land – Ma-fear-land – and we were heading to the centre of the Mafia world: Sicily.

I love the feeling of just knowing things, those times when I don't need signs or synchronicities to guide me. The signs still appear but even without them, when my intuition is firing on all cylinders, the way forward becomes very clear. Gnosis is direct knowing, not something remembered, and that is what I was experiencing. The trip to Sicily was one of those knowings. I knew that I had to be on the island in time for the new moon in Aries on 22.3.2012 as it would be taking place at exactly 2.22 degrees.

I had set off for Sicily once before, in search of an ancient spring that I knew to be important though at the time I didn't know why. I had read about it and the urge to go and find it was very strong. Even in those early days I had moments of knowing. I never made it to Sicily that time. I got as far as Sardinia and something pulled me back. The time had not been right. Now was the time.

"I've been looking at the map of Sicily. I like the sound of Siracusa," I said to Kate.

"Sirra *keys*," she joked, looking down at the neon green plastic key lying on the table. I had found the key at my feet on a recent visit to San Dominica, a short train ride down the coast from our apartment. Keys were appearing in the strangest of places.

"It says here in the Lonely Planet guide that Cicero considered it to be the most beautiful city in the ancient world.

But it's the spring I'm interested in. Listen to this: 'Just down the winding main street from the cathedral is the Fontana Aretusa where fresh water bubbles up just as it did in ancient times. Legend has it that the Goddess Artemis transformed her beautiful handmaiden Aretusa into the spring to protect her from the unwelcome attentions of the river god Alpheus'."

Kate liked the sound of the spring (and the 'key' link) so we agreed on Siracusa as our Sicilian destination. Just before we set off, my Facebook friend Angela sent me a picture of the Sicilian flag. It featured the head of Medusa. I googled 'Sicilian flag origin' and this came up:

"To have seen Italy without Sicily – is not to have seen Italy at all, as Sicily is the key to everything" – Goethe

I wasn't sure how Goethe could make such a sweeping statement but I was interested to see the key making another appearance. I couldn't understand how Sicily could be the key to everything, and I hoped Goethe was right because I'd have quite liked to have found the key to everything, but I suspected that he was talking about Sicily being the key to everything Italian and not literally everything.

We set off on our pilgrimage to Sicily. We walked to the local railway station, past the shrine of Padre Pio where a woman was kneeling piously in prayer, past the day-care centre where a young child was also on her knees, pleading with her mother not to be taken inside, past the posters illustrated with pictures of hell that were advertising a local band, and past the burned out trains and vandalised ticket machines. I walked across the rail tracks and leaned against a signpost. Somebody had scrawled 'God hates you' in English on the post. I was tempted to write 'You are God' underneath but I didn't have a permanent marker with me.

It was quite a journey from the apartment to Sicily, involving several trains and a ferry followed by another train journey, but fortunately we both enjoyed travelling. We had been blessed with another beautiful day, a pale blue sky brushed with white strokes of cloud. We passed picturesque orange and lemon orchards. Fallen fruit lay in Zen-like circles beneath many of the trees. The orchards were dotted with millions of bright yellow flowers.

But much of the west coast from Vibo Marina to Reggio Calabria where we boarded the ferry for Sicily, was ugly, marred by stacks of tatty apartment blocks. It was so sad for there was so much natural beauty in the area. The white sandy beaches and turquoise seas were magnificent, though many had been ruined by the huge amounts of debris that had been carelessly discarded on the pristine sands. A lot of historic buildings and many lives had been lost in the earthquake of 1783. Another earthquake in 1908 destroyed much of the area again and the rebuilding seemed to have been done without any care or consideration.

We took the ferry from Villa San Giovanni to Messina, Sicily. Kate and I were dressed in relatively normal clothes. All the other passengers (without exception) were dressed in black. Even the small children and the babes in arms wore black. It was a weird experience but it was because, we found out, we were sharing the ferry with a funeral party. It felt funnily appropriate, and we saw the joke that the universe manifested for us. Death and darkness made manifest.

Although we had decided on Siracusa as our destination, we stayed in a hotel in Ortygia that night. Ortygia is considered to be an island in its own right. It was attached to the city of Siracusa by 3 bridges. Only 600 metres wide and about 1km long, this could well have been the island that was referred to in my channelling. I remembered hearing,

"Canterbury is part of the geometry and there is an island. I just kept getting island. I also got 42 degrees. And Lucifer or Lucca, I'm not sure which."

Ortygia was a historical gourmet feast, packed with over 2,500 years of history and steeped in mythology. It didn't take us long to come across the Temple of Apollo where I spent the evening of 22.03.2012. As the sun and moon lined up at exactly 22 degrees and 22 seconds of Aries on the 22nd day of March, I stood alone at the ruined temple and experienced a sensation of timelessness. How strange to be standing between modern glass fronted shops selling designer goods and the ancient stone pillars of the temple that dated from the 6th-century BC. These were not the only temple pillars in town. The Cathedral of Siracusa was more like a temple than a cathedral because it had been built over the temple of Athena (around 480 BC) and the ancient columns of the temple had been integrated into the structure. Standing in the cathedral under a shaft of sunlight I was reminded that I had once owned a Spanish convent that was rumoured to have been built on the site of an Athena temple.

The next day Kate and I found the mythological fountain of Arethusa, named after the nymph of the same name. I had finally made it to this place on earth and it didn't disappoint. The fountain just felt so deeply sacred and it was buzzing with feminine power. Despite the fact that it was in a busy part of town, surrounded by buildings and people, it held its power like a ship's anchor in a storm. It was a deep, round pool with natural stone sides formed from the cliff. The whole place felt receptive and deep, deeper than the ocean, an infinite depth that I have only once experienced when looking into the eye of a human being. Looking into the deep, round pool of water felt like looking into the eye of a goddess. She looked right back at me and we recognised each other.

The Archaeological Park of Siracusa contains one of the largest Roman Amphitheatres ever constructed. It dates back to the 3rd-century AD. Like the famous Colosseum in Rome, it was used primarily for blood-curdling violent Gladiator contests. That place needed us to disperse the congealed dark energy that hung like old black cobwebs in the ethers. Kate took a photo of me beside the amphitheatre after the clearing ceremony. When I looked at the properties of the photo I noted that it had been taken on 23.03.2012 at 12.33. That's 230320121233. Those 1s, 2s and 3s were signs that we were on track.

It was our last morning in Sicily and at breakfast I was treated to a moment of sweet delight that travelling sometimes throws in my path. I was alone in the dining room of the former 'posta' a historic square building overlooking the harbour that used to house the mail workers. Breakfast was served in a beautiful old room with curved ceilings and wood framed glass doors that opened onto a small courtyard, decked in foliage. The old walnut sideboard was laden with beautiful food. Plenty of warm, freshly baked bread, large hardboiled, deep brown, free-range eggs, and red orange juice, squeezed that morning from local blood oranges. There were homemade cakes such as almond and apple and chocolate marble. Soft cheeses, spicy cold meat, fresh fruit, yoghurt and piping hot coffee filled the dining room with a cornucopia of smells.

The gentle sound of Eva Cassidy was playing quietly through the speakers. A beautiful Italian couple sat in the corner gazing into each other's eyes with love. He had long, dark wavy hair and she was a tall, slim redhead. Suddenly the receptionist entered carrying a beautifully wrapped gift. She sang a soft melody to the woman and handed her the present.

When I experience beautiful moments like that they feel like gifts. Gifts of experience are always sweeter than gifts of possessions for me. The number path certainly didn't disappoint me on that score. It showered me with incredible experiences both sweet and not so sweet!

Chapter 12

Woodspring Priory

Our pilgrimage was over. Arriving back at Stansted airport in England quite late in the evening, we booked into a hotel near the airport and were given room 111. Kate couldn't believe it, but for me it was a confirmation sign that our lightwork had been successful. It was a particularly strong sign, as on the booking form I had specified that I wanted a room on the top floor. Room 111 was on the ground floor.

The following morning we went our separate ways, Kate back to Canterbury with its links to Becket and me to the depressing housing estate to tie up the loose ends on my building project. I looked to see if there were any films on BBC iPlayer as I was tired from all the travelling and I just needed to chill. There was a film. It was the 1964 Richard Burton and Peter O'Toole film about Becket. In the corner of the screen it said 2.22.11. That was the length of the film. 2 hours, 22 minutes and 11 seconds.

The next day Kate emailed me with a photo she had taken with her iPhone as she went up the escalator in her local bookshop.

Just came up escalator in bookshop. Ahead of me - right in my face was THIS. – I took this pic. Realised I saw it at exactly 11:11. OMG!

It was of the cover of a book that had literally just been published, timed to appear for the 850th anniversary of Becket's election as archbishop of Canterbury. The book was called *Thomas* Becket, *Warrior, Priest, Rebel, Victim: A 900-Year-Old Story Retold* and was written by the well-known historian, John Guy. So it was clear that although we were back in England, Becket was still with us and was wasting no time in making his presence felt. I had already had the channelling that he was using the number 3 as a prompt but the numbers 111 and 222 were also still appearing.

I was struggling to understand what part Thomas Becket had to play in this 21st-century unfolding mystery story, so I took a book out of my local library hoping that I might be given some clues. It was a much older book than John Guy's called simply *Thomas Becket* by Frank Barlow. I opened it and a small card fell out, presumably left there by mistake by the last reader. It was handmade, less than 5 cm square and the image on the front was a single, deep pink heart. This was pure magic. As usual I turned to page 111 reasoning that if the book had a message it would be on that page. I was amused to see my name on that very page. Hilary (spelt in exactly the same way that my name is spelt) was the name of the Bishop of Chichester. And Chichester was where Kate's mum lived. It was also the birthplace of my cousin John who had died on the 22,222nd day of his life.

Are synchronicities like this miracles? They are to me. And Becket was famous for miracles. They started happening shortly after his murder. Although I found it magical to be surrounded by such incredible synchronicities, more than anything I just wanted to know why Becket was making his presence felt so many centuries after his death. He had died on December 29th 1170, more than 8 centuries earlier, yet I knew he was contacting me directly. Time was not a factor in our communication. He was operating beyond the dimension of time. I had to consider the fact that maybe I had known him during his life as Archbishop. Could I have been involved in his murder in any way? Was Kate also part of it? Could she have been there? She had already said that she kept getting an image of looking through the eyes of a monk watching the unfolding murder in the cathedral.

"It's just like I'm there," she said. "I seem to be watching it all happen."

To think that I might have witnessed or been involved in

Becket's gruesome killing was a disturbing thought but one that niggled at me. I acknowledged the thought but I didn't hold onto it. Also, I felt I had to let my 33 man, Andrew, know about the film so I emailed him.

Hi Andrew
I just got back from Italy and saw that a film about Becket was on BBC 2. It was on the day I got back. What is strange is that it is exactly 2.22.11 long. It'll only be available to watch online for a few days.

I'll be going to be in your area next week so I hope to call in and see you if you are around and if that's okay with you. There's something going on with Becket so I need to make a physical connection with your site.

Let me know if you'll be around from about 9–13th April. Hilary x

2/4/2012
Hi Hilary
Sounds great, anytime from 6pm onwards on 11th would be fine.

The address is Woodspring Farm, Kewstoke, next to Woodspring Priory on the map. Just watch out for our dopey chickens when you drive through the gates. Andrew x

PS I'm getting tingles already at the prospect, it feels like you are bringing a long extension lead to plug in and connect up to our grid...

This would be our first meeting in this life though I have no doubt that we would have known each other in previous incarnations. Although Andrew had originally thought that the priory had been built by one of the 4 knights who murdered Becket, it turned out that it had in fact been built by the grandson of Reginald Fitzurse. He was the knight that dealt the first blow to

Becket, though this was not the one that killed him. It was not by chance that the site of the priory was now in the hands of two light workers, Andrew, and his wife Victoria. They have set up a centre where they run various courses and offer short stays in nature (www.woodspringfarm.co.uk).

On my way to visit Andrew and Victoria the milometer on the car moved to 111100. That in itself was a very significant sign, but with a great deal of excitement I realised that I was finally going to find out exactly where I would be when it reached the magical 111111. I live in an unusual world. Does anyone else get excited about the numbers on their car milometer? I do. I had been driving around in a wreck of a car for years just so that I could satisfy my curiosity. I had always wanted to know where I would be when my milometer reached 111,111 miles. I had a close relationship with the numbers on it. They had spoken to me on many occasions, showing me signs and helping me along on my spiritual journey. Now it was clear that I would be on my way to Kewstoke when the milometer reached 111,111. As I was driving down a road called Queen's Way it was 111,110. As soon as I turned into the narrow country lane that led directly to the gates of Woodspring Priory, the magical 111,111 made its appearance. I had always known that I would be at a significant place on the turn of that 6 digit number 1 and I certainly wasn't disappointed. What's more, it happened at 06:06pm.

Together Andrew, Victoria and I walked around the site on which Andrew's house sat. It felt deeply sacred. I felt the presence of an ancient guardian from long, long ago, well before the building of the priory in the 12th-century. There were 3 springs on the land. They needed honouring and protecting, as did the well on the adjoining plot. I had a strong sense of connection with Rome but also Spain. I also felt a link to Wells Cathedral and Stanton Drew stone circle so I knew I needed to look at the alignments later. There were rumours of a tunnel that emerged several miles away in a place called Monks steps. This was very likely as many of these ancient sites were connected to underground tunnels and caverns. Andrew told me that a reliquary had been found in the wall of the priory that contained Becket's blood, but he didn't know what had happened to it. I vowed to find it.

We reached the fire pit in the middle of the garden shortly before sunset and we had a small ceremony. The pit was not quite finished. It had been waiting for that day for the 3 of us to come together in our physical forms to initiate the healing of Woodspring and to the connecting places on the earth grid. The stars shone bright and clear in the spring night sky. The 3 of us stood in an east/west alignment and tuned in energetically to Kate. She texted me later to tell me that she had felt the transmission of a strong image of keys.

When I returned home I then checked the latitude of Stanton Drew: 51.36. Kewstoke: 51.36. I then saw that Wells and Stanton Drew stone circle were equidistant from Kewstoke. The neat geometry of these places confirmed my earlier intuitive revelation. I looked at the alignments. It didn't take long to discover that they were between Andrew's priory, Rome and Granada. The number 11:11 had once led me to buy an old convent in the Spanish province of Granada. It had been a school of illustrious studies in the 17th-century, linked to the University of Granada. I was clearly working on the same planetary energy lines that I had worked on several years earlier (see The *11:11 Code* by Hilary H. Carter)

A few nights later on Friday 13th April I had a dream:

There was a huge auditorium. People were gathering for a concert. The door was locked. I had a key so I unlocked it with a Yale key and entered with Victoria and Andrew. We walked through the door and behind there was a square opening. It was a spring deep in the ground. The auditorium was square. The spring dated to Roman times.

Chapter 13

The Reliquary

Having visited the site of the priory, it was time to visit the reliquary that had been found in the wall. It was held in the museum of Somerset in the town of Taunton. A few days later I drove to Taunton and I parked the car. It was 11:33am. My parking ticket expired at 13.33. Peals of melodic bells rang out as I entered the museum, which was located inside Taunton castle, a Grade 1 Listed Scheduled Ancient Monument standing at the heart of Somerset's county town. It is Taunton's most important secular historic monument. It was Saturday afternoon so the bell ringing was obviously because somebody was getting married in a nearby church. Kate had been right about the sign of the bells. We were being spoken to by both numbers and bells.

The county museum was amazing. Having located the glass cabinet that contained the reliquary I stood and tried to tune in to any messages that might be relayed to me. I was also linking in consciousness with Kate. I kept getting the word 'fire'. Kate was given the word 'key' again.

Then a small child appeared out of nowhere, and came and stood next to me. He observed me looking at the beautiful stone object that had housed the wooden cup of Becket's blood. I looked down at his sweet little face. "Jesus died on the cross," he said as he looked directly into my eyes. That's all he said. Then he promptly turned and walked off. I read the inscription beside the relic.

The Kewstoke Reliquary. The relics of saints had powerful religious significance for the faithful. This limestone reliquary was found in Saint Paul's church, Kewstoke. It held a wooden cup which was believed to contain the blood of St Thomas A

Becket. The reliquary may originally have belonged to the nearby Woodspring priory which was dedicated to St Thomas A Becket. C.1300 Kewstoke. St Paul's church.

The wooden cup of blood is believed to have belonged to the monks at Woodspring, but when the monasteries were destroyed by Henry VIII, the monks hid it in the wall of the nearby church for safety. It remained hidden for centuries until 1849 when renovation work on the church revealed this treasure.

The energy in this particular part of the museum was tangible. I wandered round looking for a key. Kate had been given this symbol more than once, so maybe there was a key somewhere in the museum that would have meaning. I then had a mind imprint given. The key was symbolic, not literal. What item in the room was the key? On the shelf next to the cup that contained Becket's blood was a ham stone case. Nobody knew the origins of this case that would have been used for heart burials. It had been found in an unnamed and unknown Somerset church. It was marked with the number 10. Next to it was item 11. This was also a heart case, the only 2 heart cases in the museum. "Is the heart the key?" I asked. At that point there was a crack of thunder from the atmospheric sound track that was playing in the background. I took it to be my answer: Yes. This was the second time there had been a link between Becket and the heart. I had kept the small card that had fallen from the Becket library book and it stood on my altar.

A couple of weeks later my Facebook friend Angela sent me details of the first Italian crop circle of 2012. It appeared on 5/5. In the very centre of the circle was a pentagon. That could be referring to the Pentagon in the USA as I knew that the Pentagon was located at 38 degrees of latitude. So was the Thomas Becket Cathedral at Marsala. I began to get the feeling that I needed to visit Marsala, which was quite annoying as I had only just come back from Sicily. I just hoped that the feeling would pass.

Chapter 14

The passage of Venus

Once again I was experiencing a 'knowing'. I just knew I had to go to Turin. It wasn't a thought that I had to go, neither was purely an intuitive feeling. It was simply this mysterious force of knowing that surrounded and permeated my entire being and would not (nor could not) be ignored because it grew in intensity day by day. This strange feeling was happening to me more and more often. I also had the knowing that I had to be there on 6/6 for that was the date of the passage of Venus. The passage of Venus across the face of the Sun happens every 104 years. A Venus transit is an astronomical event where the planet Venus passes between the Earth and the Sun. Venus was very important to the Mayans. They saw it as a sister planet to Earth and one ancient Mayan prophecy says that the new world of consciousness would be born on the occasion of the Venus Passage in June, 2012.

The last Venus transit had been in June 2004 as they always come in pairs eight years apart. It was only in hindsight that I realised I had bought my Spanish convent on the Venus transit of 2004. The number 11:11 had led me to buy the Spanish convent followed by a French convent in 2007 and I tell those stories in my books *The 11:11 Code* (Spanish convent) and *No Name No Number* (French convent).

Somehow the visit to Turin would be linking to an important task that I would be involved in on 12/12/12. I just knew it. These moments of knowing come from beyond the mind and the personal 'me'. I had no idea what my task was to be, nor did I have any idea where I would be on 12/12/12. The incoming light encoded frequencies bombarding the earth during the eclipses and planetary transits of 2012 would be ushering in the next stage of human DNA activation. I was guessing my task might be to make preparations for those codes to enter but I would just have to wait and see where the signs would send me.

This pressure to go to Turin was so powerful that I surrendered and I went online to book my flight ticket. The number signs were everywhere. There was no way I could ignore them. When I went to find out the cost of flights, British Airways emailed me their quote (the only quote I got) at 11:01. I booked the ticket there and then. My e-ticket was mailed to my inbox within minutes. It arrived at exactly 11:11. The following day BA sent another email asking me if I would like to upgrade. That was sent at 1:11pm. I photographed the laptop screen for the first 2 number signs. I couldn't find proof of the time of the 3rd email so I right clicked on 'properties' and the number 6-6666-666666666666 appeared in the address bar followed by 66666666-6666-6666-666666666666. I have to say that is the most spectacular line-ups of the number 6 I have ever encountered. Maybe the number 6 was appearing because of the 6/6 date. Naturally I have the photo of the 6 phenomenon screen. I was gradually getting into the habit of photographing a lot of my bizarre number synchronicities as they were becoming more and more unbelievable. Being able to retrieve pictorial evidence of my number miracles was a way of assuring myself (and others) that these incredible synchronicities were actually taking place and were not a figment of my imagination. Whenever I am accused of exaggerating my number synchronicities I simply bring out the photos as evidence. I can quite understand why people would doubt me because the way that numbers appear in my life is beyond belief. They're utterly staggering.

The number signs for Turin were not only the repeated numbers 1 and 6 but there were lots of 2s, 22s and 222s. Also 1s and 2s in number patterns such as 1221, 121212 and so on. I knew that the number 2 was Kate's number so I asked her if she would like to come with me. I would not influence Kate either way. The decision to come or not to come had to be hers and hers alone. I had such a strong feeling that she was meant to join me. I was sure she would simply see the signs and take the leap of faith. Just after emailing her to invite her along my mobile rang. It was from the number 1212121212, and yes, I also have the photo of the date and number of this call. However, after considering it for a while, Kate decided not to join me. She said that she would prefer to connect with me in spirit by being at her local abbey on 6/6, a few hundred metres from her house in Canterbury, England. Saint Augustine's Abbey dates back to AD 597 and it sits just outside the city walls.

I was both surprised and slightly bemused by her decision so I emailed her and asked her whether any numbers had arisen around her decision to be at the abbey. They hadn't. Having made the decision to be at the abbey I asked whether any numbers had appeared to confirm it to be in alignment with divine will. They hadn't. Maybe her mind had influenced her decision. My own mind had tried to sway my decision because to be in Turin for 6/6 meant:

- Changing the date of my return to my home in France.
- Travelling on an extremely busy English Bank Holiday as 6/6 coincided with the Queen's Jubilee celebrations.
- Paying for the flight, the hotels, and the transport to and from the airports.

Of course Hilary didn't want all that bother and expense but I did not allow my mind to hold precedence over the signs, nor did Hari (my Divine Self) allow Hilary (my ego Self) to influence matters. My decision was based on No Mind.

As soon as Kate had made her decision and I knew I would be alone in Turin I had a dream:

I was in a house and behind the walls there were wide partitions filled with rats. I went outside into the long garden, at the end of which was a shallow, muddy swimming pool. I waded through the pool to the sea beyond. There were large waves (coming in pairs), but they were going in the wrong direction. Instead of heading for the shore they were heading out to sea.

I don't dream that often, but when I do they are normally crammed with symbolism so I took note. I had a distinct feeling that this dream was linked to the work I was to do in Turin. Knowing that I would be travelling alone, I continued to make my travel arrangements. I've booked hundreds of hotels in my time so I found it very strange to see that my booking for my particular hotel was accompanied by its longitude and latitude. That was a first – 45.073 latitude. My convent in France was located on the 45.0667 degrees of latitude. That's one hell of a close connection. Not only that, the postcode of the hotel was 10122 and the phone number ended in 22 6 22. I didn't tell Kate. It was not my place to influence her. Her decision not to join me had to be based on her own truth.

Chapter 15

Dracula's Castle

It took me a while for it to sink in that I would be travelling to Turin alone. I just had this very strong feeling that this particular work needed other people to be involved. I wasn't worried, just slightly puzzled. However, it wasn't long before my intuitive feeling was proved to be right because suddenly my friend Mike Handcock and his business partner Dave were brought into the picture. The week before the Turin trip they contacted me to say that they were on a world tour and they were in England. I don't see them often as Mike lives in New Zealand and Dave in Singapore, so I jumped at the chance to meet up. We met in Exeter in Devon and visited the cathedral. There was a poster on the cathedral door advertising a talk on 'The Life of Thomas Becket'. Inside the cathedral I was shown a Becket boss that dated from the 1300s.

"How long will you be in England for?" I asked Mike and Dave as we sat down for a hearty English breakfast in a beautiful Georgian mansion, now a pub.

"Just two more days. Then we're going to Romania," said Mike.

"Romania? That's a bit random. Why are you going there?" I asked.

"For a board meeting," said Dave. "We're thinking out the box. Board meetings don't have to take place in an office, they can happen anywhere. And I've always wanted to visit Dracula's castle so we thought we could combine our meeting with visiting a place I have always wanted to visit."

"Good idea," I replied.

When I returned home later that day I looked at the map to see exactly where the castle was located:

Bran castle. 45 degrees of latitude (Wikipedia).

45 degrees, exactly the same as Turin. The 45 degrees of latitude is extremely significant. The 45 degrees of latitude was involving Turin, my convent in France (see my book *No Name No Number*) and Dracula's castle as all 3 locations were on this latitude. Turin is the connecting point of the triangles of black and white magic on the planet. The black magic triangle connects Turin to London and San Francisco. These cities are believed to be united by lines of negative energy. The white magic triangle connects Turin with Lyons and Prague. These cities are believed to be united by lines of positive energy. Rather worryingly I read that Turin is rumoured to be the location of the gates of Hell.

I could see what the universe was doing with Mike and Dave. It was adjusting to the fact that Kate wouldn't be joining me in Turin. I believe that we have free will within the play of consciousness so she could make her own decisions and choose not to go. The universe then adapted to this. I knew that the darkness of the Vatican would pale in comparison with the gates of hell. I had already started preparing my physical body to be clear enough to handle the energy. Because the work in Turin would be so intense for my physical body, Mike and Dave had an important job to do too. Their task was to release the intensity of the power of the darkness that was permeating the earth in Romania. They had to install a column of light. Doing this would facilitate my work at the gates of hell. I emailed them to explain the *real* reason for their planned visit to Romania! Clearance work at this level does, however, attract the attention of the dark forces that will do their utmost to prevent it. They had already made their presence felt but I knew that they would not succeed in preventing the anchoring of the light.

It would take 6 days to do the 6/6 work, 3 days before midnight on 5th/6th June and 3 days afterwards, a total of 144 hours. 144 is the number of ascension. Within these 144 hours there would be an eclipsed full moon.

I had to have a link with someone in London on 6/6 and it needed to be at midday. Fortunately I knew exactly how to go about this. At that time I was a member of a group known as the Children of the Sun. This group accepts members from all paths that lead to unity, love and the truth of the Divine Presence as our inherent nature. I posted a request on their forum.

On 6/6 I will be in Turin for the Venus transit. Not only is Turin at the connection point of light and dark on the planet but it is on the mystical 45 degrees of latitude. I need to connect with a light worker in London at noon on 6/6 in order to unblock a major part of the earth grid on that day. A 12 minute connection, 6 minutes before noon and 6 minutes after. I will be holding the light at the Piazza Statuto. Could one of you who lives in London help me in this work?

I knew who was to help me in this work even before she posted her response. I'm sure that Rose had no idea that she responded to my request at exactly 6 seconds after 6pm: 06:00:06.

I packed for my journey to the gates of hell. I was flying out of London on Tuesday 5th June and spending the night of 4th June with my sister who lived in a 14th-century house within the walls of Salisbury Cathedral Close in Wiltshire, England. As I drove to the cathedral late in the evening, my route was lit by beacons. It was wonderful. On top of the ancient site of Melbury Hill I saw a blazing fire. 2,012 beacons of fire were lit on all the high places of the UK on the 4th June 2012 as it was the Queen's jubilee. The beacons may have been intended for the Queen but at another level they were for my own inner Goddess. I really felt like queen in my own right, my path lit with fire. This felt so symbolic. It reminded me of standing at the relics in the museum of Somerset when Kate was given the word 'key' and I was given the word 'fire'. And of course I noted the connection between fire and hell.

Chapter 16

The Gates of Hell

I drove through the 14th-century stone gate and parked the car by my sister's house. I had set the trip meter on zero when I set off. Now it read 111.1. That meant that my sister and I were living exactly 111.1 miles away from each other. As I slept within the ancient walls of Salisbury Cathedral Close that night I had a visionary dream. I briefed Mike and Dave with my findings.

Dear Mike and Dave,
All this was all presented to me in last night's dream. Your work begins at 6pm on 5th June. Do not eat anything after 6pm and drink only water. Don't panic, it's only a 12 hour fast. The ego might not like it but work of this nature cannot be done with ego present.

Bathe or shower between 6-7pm in warm water. Pay particular attention to immersing the head in water. Put on clean clothes. Preferably white but certainly not black.

Prepare your pentagram. It needs to be put in a flame (fire or a lighter) and as you hold it in the flame say, "In the name of (your chosen protector) I demand the protection of the Christ light."

Then immerse the pentagram in water. Hold it in both hands (closed hands) and chant the mantra Om Namah Shivaya 3 times thereby imbuing it with the energy of Babaji. (Om Namah Shivaya is the mantra of Babaji, the immortal yogi of the Himalayas.) Place the pentagram around your neck. If you feel guided to doing any more protective work, follow your inner guidance.

The hours after 6pm can be spent in quiet contemplation or walking in nature. Hanging out with other people is a no-no. The ceremony proper starts at 6 minutes to midnight and ends at 6 minutes past. It must be exactly 12 minutes as 12 is the relevant number here, not 11. You need to be near water for this, a spring, river, lake, well, fountain or stream.

You must protect your temples as this is the main point of entry for dark entities. I normally rub mine with circular movements using sacred ash or holy water. Use the index finger and silently chant as you rub. You could use frankincense oil. You MUST do the temple protection. I also smoke my entire aura with good quality incense or dried sage leaves.

Your link is between Venus and the underworld. You are placing a column of light anywhere within the vicinity of the castle. You don't need to be within the walls as the underground tunnel system is vast.

At 6 minutes to midnight begin chanting the mantra out loud. It needs to be chanted 25 times in these 12 minutes. If you don't have a mala use 25 sweets/stones/matches to keep count.

Intention is everything. Know that you are the physical connection between Venus and the earth deep under your feet. You will be used as conduits. Exactly HOW you anchor this column is your decision to make. Follow your intuition.

I know this is quite a lot to take on but the fact that you are on the 45 degrees during the Venus transit is the confirmation sign that you are involved in this work. You are preparing the path for my contribution to the ascension. I will be continuing the work at noon on 6/6 with the help of a lightworker in London. My task ends at 12.06pm. 12 hours 12 minutes from the start of your ceremony to the end of mine.

Let me know if you have any questions. I leave for Turin later today and I might not be able to get online for a few days so I might be out of contact. But you can always try texting me if it's urgent. Please don't share any of the details of this with anyone until the work is completed on June 21st.

Thank you for stepping up to this task brothers. I love you. Hx

Having briefed Mike and Dave, I flew to Turin, touching down exactly 11 weeks after the spring equinox. I booked into my hotel just around the corner from The Piazza Statuto, the very centre of Turin's Satanic energy system. Within this square is the Fontana del Frejus, a stone monument that commemorates those who died during the building of the Frejus tunnel that connects Italy and France. The monument depicts men in loincloths buried in rocks, their faces in varying degrees of agony. It's not a pretty sight and it has a strong link with death, suffering and dark underground tunnels, quite fitting for a monument at a doorway of darkness. It has been erected at the spot where thousands had been executed on the gallows in days gone by. Nearby is a manhole cover above a series of underground tunnels. It is the modern day entrance to the sewers but it is also widely believed to lead to the gates of hell. I thought back to my dream about the rats and wondered how many there would be beneath my feet. There is a lot going on underground in Turin. There are tourist tours of the underground passages. It is also possible to take a tour of demonic statues, the street where the famous seer Nostradamus once lived and churches such as the Misericordia, where prisoners were given last rites before execution. Tourists can view a list of those put to death, the black hoods that they wore, and the glass used for their last drink. Needless to say, I was not tempted by these tours.

I stood at the base of the monument. The water was stagnant, smelly and full of rubbish. On the top of the monument was a statue of an angel with a star on top of its head. The star was placed so that 2 of the points of the star were upright. That is the dark way. It is said that this figure represents the image of Lucifer, the lost angel, banished after his rebellion against God. The energy was cold and clammy like the green gunge I had seen in the former funeral parlour that I had once lived in. I did some preparatory work. I walked around the statue 11 times. I placed my raw sapphire in the water of the fountain to charge the water and I said some prayers.

As 5pm approached I began to prepare myself for the link

with Mike and Dave. I recited more prayers and aligned my energy with those on the non-physical level who were using my physical body for this work. I felt safe in the knowledge that Mike and Dave were holding the space in Transylvania.

Having done the preparatory work it was my intention to be back at the gates of hell at noon on the following day (6/6) to seal the door. That was Hilary's expectation. I was soon to discover that the universe had other ideas.

Chapter 17

The Egyptian Temple

I slept surprisingly well that night. I often do when I am in a fasted state. I had a dream about a ball of string. I dropped it and it unravelled itself in a very unusual way. It went through the window of a palace in a perfectly straight line.

I left the hotel early on the morning of 6/6, intending to go for a wander and then head back to the statue by noon. As I stepped out of the hotel lobby into the street a huge number 66 was flashing on and off on the illuminated display board. 66 was not subtle in its appearance that day. Everywhere I walked I was distracted by the date flashing on and off on the large digital clocks. The 6/6 flashing was interspersed with the number 23 as that was the temperature. 23 is a very unstable number, the number of breakdown and breakthrough.

It wasn't just the numbers 23 and 66 talking to me. The sign of the single eye was also everywhere, just like it was in Rome. In fact it seemed to be appearing even more frequently than the number signs. It was a beautiful morning. The sunshine was bright and the skies were clear. There was a gentle breeze blowing softly through the city.

Turin was an interesting city to wander around. I walked over countless grills on the pavements giving me glimpses of the underground tunnels and passageways that were below the city. I had no destination in mind, I would simply allow myself to explore and make my way back to the monument before noon. I was feeling slightly fragile because I was still in a fasted state so I walked slowly.

By about 10:30am I reached the cathedral, dedicated to John the Baptist. I climbed 2 steps up to the first level and then 11 steps up to the cathedral itself. I was just wandering around looking at the paintings when suddenly I came across the shroud of Turin. I had completely forgotten that it was kept in there. I started when I saw this large cabinet that contained the shroud and I had one of my goose pimples all over moments. I guess this shroud could be examined, carbon dated, x-rayed and photographed but for me I don't need that. My body was the barometer of truth. Every cell of my being said that this was the actual cloth that Jesus body had been wrapped in.

The shroud is owned by the Vatican and it had been kept in a French convent in Chambery for many years before being moved to Turin. Chambery is on the 45 degrees of latitude. It is considered to be a mystical latitude because it is exactly half way between the pole and the equator.

I sat for a while in front of the shroud as hordes of tourists on organised tours came and went, looking at the shroud for a few minutes and then moving on. Gradually the cathedral completely emptied until I was the only person left sitting there. I was approached by an elderly woman, one of the cathedral guides. Unbidden and unsought, I was given masses of information about the shroud and the cathedral.

"The shroud is in there," she said pointing to the wooden cabinet inside a glass case. "It's very long because it is stored in an unfolded state."

She had all the facts at her fingertips. Jesus must have been over 177cms. That's tall for those times and it reminded me of Thomas who was known to be extremely tall.

Behind there," she continued, pointing to a forbidding black marble doorway to my right, "the royal family would enter. They had a private passageway that led directly from the palace to the cathedral because the royal palace is right next door."

I recalled my dream of the string the night before.

By far the most interesting thing was under the cathedral, the ruins of three 5th- and 6th-century churches, which had been demolished in 1498 to make way for the existing cathedral.

"I love old ruins," I said to the guide as we stood looking at the piles of stones.

"Then you must go to the Egyptian museum. There is an old Egyptian temple in there. It's complete, transported from Egypt. It was presented to the city of Turin in 1966."

I found it highly significant that she should know the date of the arrival of the temple. 1966. I couldn't ignore the synchronicity of the double 6.

"And it's not far to the museum. Let me show you where it is."

We stepped outside and the guide took around the corner me to the gates of the palace. It was literally adjoining the cathedral. There were lots of golden Medusa's heads on the railings. That was a clear link with Sicily because of the appearance of Medusa's head on Sicily's flag. I was also interested to learn that Da Vinci had painted the head of Medusa early on in his life but sadly the paintings have been lost.

I didn't think I would have time to visit the museum before heading back to the gates of hell but I thought that maybe I could visit later in the day.

"What is the time?" I asked as I thought it might be time to head towards the gates of hell. She pointed up to the flashing clock on the stone facade of a nearby shop. I stared in disbelief because it was 11:11am.

I kept 'Hilary' out of the way and went with the flow. Despite the fact that 'Hilary' had been expecting to be at the gates of hell, I realised that I was being guided (quite literally by a guide) to the Egyptian museum and the 11:11 time prompt was confirming the divinity of the guidance. Non-attachment is required on the path of number and that includes non-attachment to expectations. As I crossed the square, heading for the museum, preparations were being made for a jazz festival. My way was blocked by a large van that was unloading sound equipment. On the side was written 'ALPHA AND OMEGA' in large capital letters. I certainly was dealing with source energy.

"I am Alpha and Omega, the first and the last." Revelations 1:11.

As soon as I arrived at the museum I saw the sign pointing towards the temple. GPS isn't needed when guidance is this clear. The temple was the place where I was to link with Rose. She had such a perfect name for this type of work as a rose is symbolic of love.

The Temple of Ellesija had been offered to Italy by Egypt in 1966 at a time when it was endangered by the rising water of the Nile because of the construction of the Aswan dam. It had been brought to Italy in its complete state. To reach it I had to walk through the gallery of Egyptian statues. Rushes of Egyptian energy engulfed me and I had to concentrate on the contact of my feet with the floor as I could easily have left my body. I had experienced so many Egyptian lives that my consciousness was drifting back to those times. I breathed in deeply and exhaled completely several times, grounding myself firmly in the here and now. Thank goodness for my knowledge of yoga breathing.

The temple was full of people, but within minutes of my arrival they had all disappeared. I found myself completely alone inside a genuine Egyptian temple in the heart of Turin. Numbers, signs and synchronicities certainly lead me to some interesting places. I noticed that several pentacles had been carved into the stone walls. They looked more recent than the hieroglyphs.

I was thankful that on my last visit to Babaji's ashram I had been given the sacred string from the lingham of the Havan fire. I wore it around my wrist, knowing that I was divinely protected at the highest level. Such grace. I anointed my temples and wrists and upper chakras with lotus oil that I had bought in Mysore and began the work.

From deep in the recesses of my mind came the name Alice Bailey. I had studied her books some years earlier and had been in the habit of using the Great Invocation on a daily basis:

From the point of Light within the Mind of God
Let light stream forth into the minds of men.
Let Light descend on Earth.
From the point of Love within the Heart of God
Let love stream forth into the hearts of men.
May Christ return to Earth.
From the centre where the Will of God is known
Let purpose guide the little wills of men —
The purpose which the Masters know and serve.
From the centre which we call the race of men
Let the Plan of Love and Light work out.
And may it seal the door where evil dwells.
Let Light and Love and Power
restore the Plan on Earth.

I repeated it 3 times, then the 23rd psalm and then my mantra Om Namah Shiva. Several days later I realised the perfection of the invocation: 'May it seal the door where evil dwells...' That is exactly what the work in Turin involved.

As soon as I finished the crowds returned. It didn't matter. The job was done and nothing and nobody could undo it. I was kept in peace during the ceremonial work and within minutes of finishing the crowds returned. Only one person had entered during the 12 minutes from 11:54 to 12:06pm (a woman) and I felt she represented the energy of Rose as she connected with me from London. The lone female tourist had entered and left in complete silence.

As I stepped out of the temple I unlocked my phone. The key pad flashed as if to tell me that something had been unlocked, like a switch that triggered something. I remembered Kate's son asking about the switch for the outside light. At that time I had no idea of the significance of that statement, but I had filed the moment and now I was beginning to understand its significance. I thought that 12 minutes seemed like such a short time to be having such a profound effect on the energy of the earth, but I realised that I was simply being used as a switch. That was all. The role of the Light Servers on the planet at this time in our evolution is to consciously receive and physically integrate the incoming light encodements. That is what I was doing in Turin. My physical body was being used as a switch to encode the earth grid on the 45 degrees of latitude.

Chapter 18

Jendra

Just before I left the museum I returned to the temple for one last look. As I entered I was joined by a man. Like me, he was alone. I looked at him. Our eyes met and as soon as they did so I felt a rush of energy rather like the feeling you get when you stand a little too close to the edge of a railway platform as an express train passes at full speed through the station. Jendra! I recognised him immediately from one of my Egyptian lives. Fancy meeting him in an Egyptian temple of all places. I didn't feel able to ask him if he remembered me from Egypt. Instead I asked him to take my photo. Maybe looking at me through the camera might jog a distant recognition from within the recesses of his memory.

"I'll stand here right in front of the altar."

"Okay," he said, lining me up and looking at me through the lens. "Ready…1, 2, 3."

He captured that moment in time. The properties tab on the photo recorded the numbers of that moment: 11:33am on the day of the Venus transit. (It was actually 12:33 but the camera was set on British summer time.)

"I'll do another one just in case that one doesn't come out. Ready…1, 2, 3…"

Again the moment was captured.

"Yes, that's fine, thanks," I said. "But it should have been 6 instead of 1, 2, 3. 1, 2, 3, 4, 5, 6."

He looked at me with a quizzical expression.

"Well today is 6/6," I explained.

"Yes," he said, "…and?"

He obviously wasn't yet tuned into the world of number.

"It doesn't matter…" My voice trailed away.

I turned and walked away, but it didn't matter because if he had meant to recognise me he would have. Much later in the day I realised that he had said 6 after all. He had said 1, 2, 3 before each photo. 1+2+3=6 and he had said it twice. Also 123 plus 123 is 6 digits. There will not be another Venus transit in my lifetime. There will not be another 6/6 ceremony leading up to 2012. But I will always remember that brief encounter in the Temple of Ellesija with a certain degree of poignancy.

I strolled slowly away from the museum reflecting on that strange encounter with Jendra. For a brief moment I thought about going back in and finding him but it didn't feel right to do that. I reminded myself to be in the moment and not to get caught in the 'what ifs' of the mind. Besides which, I was starving because I had kept myself in a fasted state for the healing work. Now that the work was done I could eat. On my way back to the hotel I passed a small takeaway restaurant. 'Indian street food', said the sign outside.

They had my favorite meal, mung dhal and chapattis so I ordered a portion and sat down to wait for it to be heated up. I got talking to one of the Indian men whilst I was waiting.

"I've been to India," I said, "and today I'm wearing my Indian bracelet. Look. It says Om Namah Shiva in silver metal."

I showed him the Babaji bracelet that I had bought at a small yoga centre in Medicine Hat, Canada when I had travelled the 111 degree of longitude several years earlier. He called out something in Indian to his friend in the kitchen and he came out.

"Look at her bracelet. It's the same as yours."

The second man looked at my wrist and smiled, his eyes wide in wonder. "Yes, it's Om Namah Shiva the same as mine."

He reached under the counter and handed me his bracelet.

"I can't wear it while I'm cooking so I have to leave it under here while I'm preparing food. Health and safety regulations you know."

His was a battered replica of my bracelet and obviously much older than mine. I examined it carefully. Apart from some missing trim it was exactly the same in every way.

"Babaji," I whispered.

"Yes, Babaji," he replied quietly. We didn't need to say anything else. I knew that this encounter in a street cafe in Turin on 6/6 was the immortal yogi making his presence felt.

Within 24 hours of the 'light switch' in the Egyptian temple, storms began raging over Europe. Flights out of Turin were delayed and I had one of the worst landings I have ever endured into London's Gatwick airport. I arrived in winds of 70mph. I'm sure that this was due to the ceremonies that Mike, Dave and I had performed. During their ceremony in Romania a series of coloured lights appeared above Dracula's castle and Mike managed to capture this on video. They were the colours of the first 5 chakras and appeared at 12:12.

Exactly 11 days after 6/6, on June 17th 2012, a crop circle appeared just outside Turin. It looked exactly like an eye complete with eyelashes. The symbol of an eye was definitely trying to get through to me.

Chapter 19

The Relics

I have always had the feeling that I was to work with 3 convents in this life. Somehow the numbers seemed to guide me towards old religious buildings. During the last 10 years I had bought a Spanish convent and then a French convent. Maybe the third and final one would be in Italy. However, it was already June 2012 and no Italian convent had appeared. I was slightly bemused about the third convent because I knew that the 3 convents were all linked to 12/12/12, and I was running out of time to find it. There were 12 gate openings before the 'day of ascension', which was December 21st 2012. The crystal grid around the earth was being activated in phases, each taking place on a triple date: 1/1/1 through to 12/12/12. Each of these dates carries numeric light codes that open and activate each of the 12 major pentacle facets of the new earth template.

I had to remind myself that everything was unfolding perfectly. My Divine Self was in control of my life and she knew better than Hilary how to run things.

The work in Turin was finished so it was finally time to return home to my French convent. I had managed to get hold of a copy of John Guy's newly published book about Becket. According to John Guy, Becket's mother was unusually pious. She was a devotee of the cult of the Blessed Virgin Mary to whom she taught her son to pray. At about the age of 10, Becket was sent to the Augustinian Priory at Merton in Surrey to be educated. What particularly interested me was the fact that the monks at Merton were intensely dedicated to the same cult as his mother. There is no doubt that Becket would have been influenced by the beliefs of these monks. It was a Goddess cult. And I was working with the Divine Feminine energy...

I needed to make contact with Becket's relics before I left England for France, so I phoned Kate to ask if I could stay with her for a few days. I explained that I would be on my way to the cross channel ferry because I was going back to France.

"I just want to go to the cathedral before I leave. I want to see Becket's relics."

"Okay. Let's arrange to be inside the cathedral at 4pm because that's the time he was killed."

"Okay, great, I'll meet you at the entrance at 3.30pm," I replied.

When I turned up at the gate to Canterbury Cathedral the place was heaving with tourists. The queue stretched back all the way up the street. I knew I would never make the front of the queue by 4pm so I called Kate on her mobile and asked her to come out and meet me on the street. She was already inside the cathedral. As a resident of Canterbury she had a pass that allowed her to visit whenever she liked, unlike visitors who had to pay £10 each to enter.

"Don't worry about the queue. There's another entrance that the tourists don't know about," she said when we met. "Follow me."

I followed her down the road, but the secret entrance was locked.

"That's a shame. I wanted to be at the relics by 4pm," I said.

She looked puzzled. "What relics?" she asked.

"Becket's relics. The ones in the cathedral," I replied.

"But there are no relics in the cathedral. There's the place where the shrine to Becket used to be and there's the place where he was murdered but that's all. Anything of Becket that might have been there in the past has long gone. Henry VII saw to that when he destroyed the monasteries in 1536."

I was disappointed. I had come all the way to Canterbury because of this urge to connect with his relics only to discover that there were none.

"I wish you had told me that there were no relics before I came all this way."

"I suppose I just assumed that you knew. Never mind," said Kate as we continued walking along the street away from the hordes of tourists. "We can go to the spot where he was murdered and tune in to him there. I do know of another entrance only it's quite a walk. Oh, look at that. It says, 'Catholic Church of St Thomas of Canterbury'."

We stopped by an unassuming little church set back from the narrow road. Outside was a wooden plaque with details of the times of the services. Kate's mouth fell open in shock.

"Look. Look what it says."

I read the inscription.

"In the Martyrs' Chapel inside this church are relics of St. Thomas of Canterbury. So there *are* relics after all. Why didn't you tell me about these ones?" I asked.

"I had no idea they were here. I have lived in Canterbury for decades and I have never known about them. Like most people I focus on the cathedral. That's what Canterbury is famous for. Millions of people file through there every year to see where Becket's shrine used to be and only a few hundred metres away there are these actual relics, but hardly anybody knows about them."

"Including you…"

"Yes. Come on, let's go in."

We entered cautiously and silently. In sharp contrast to the packed cathedral, the little church of St Thomas was completely empty. The relics were in a small side chapel. As we approached the cabinet I came out in goose pimples just like I had in Turin Cathedral by the Turin shroud. There was a small piece of Becket's bone (probably a finger) and a piece of his vestment. There was a plaque with 3 black birds on it that I later learned were choughs, members of the crow family. Maybe the black birds were on his coat of arms because a chough is an Old World bird, also known as…a beckit. Kate and I sat on the hard wooden chairs in preparation for meditation.

"Okay, let's have the message Thomas," I joked as we sat down. Then I jumped out of my skin as the bell tolled loudly 3 times. I burst out laughing. That was just so incredible, an instantaneous answer to my question.

"The number 3! Becket, you're so funny…"

The time was quarter to 4, so the bells had tolled 3 times to indicate that. They tolled once to indicate quarter past the hour, twice for half past and 3 times for quarter to. On the hour itself they tolled the number of the hour.

Being so close to the relics I received a channelling.

The 3 in the current situation refers to you, me and Kate. The 3 of us are working together. We create a triangle. I will send communications to you in dreams. Take note of your dreams. You followed my guidance by coming to Canterbury. The urge to come was impressed upon you by my consciousness communicating directly with yours. We have work to do. It is not finished yet.

It was now clear that Becket was indeed the third person that had been referred to in my channelling. I remember what I had said to Kate:

"I was given Rome and Sicily and that 3 people are involved in Italy. It could be you, me and Andrew or a third person we have not yet met. It's even possible that the third person could be Becket himself."

The following day Kate and I explored the local Knights Templar churches near Canterbury. We were standing at the door of a particularly isolated country church. It was a beautiful summer's day, but the church was locked, so I was trying to peer in through the window.

"Look," said Kate. "Turn around."

I turned, and there between 2 telegraph poles that formed a perfect number 11 was a white horse. It was standing stock still staring at us.

"Oh my goodness," I said, "what a beauty."

"It's staring at us."

"I know. It's as if he's trying to impart a message to us."

"I think white horses are something to do with bravery. And of course they're in the book of Revelation."

I saw heaven standing open and there before me was a white horse, whose rider is called Faithful and True. Book of Revelation 19:11

It was my Facebook friend Angela who gave me another answer. She informed me that Medusa had a son who was a white horse – Pegasus, the winged white horse of mythology. I recalled all the Medusa plaques on the gates of the Palace of Turin and wondered what the link was. Maybe there was a clue in the mythology.

My life seemed to be one synchronicity after another. I was aware of being fully alive, as if every atom of my being was buzzing with electrical energy. I realised that the signs indicated that I was connected to the energy stream, like going down a water flume. When you're in the current you need do nothing. You're led, taken. The challenge is to get into the current. The current is the energy and for me the numbers are the guidance.

Chapter 20

France

After making contact with Becket's relics, I set off to France. I checked my Facebook before I left and was rather alarmed to see that Mike Handcock had updated his profile picture. In the new photo he was wearing…a trilby hat. I hoped that wasn't linked to my dream in any way.

I had replaced my old banger with a newer car once it had reached 111,111 miles so I was quite looking forward to the drive down in a new and reliable vehicle. Canterbury is not far from Dover so I took the ferry from Dover to Calais. It was called The Pride of Canterbury. As I drove off the ferry in Calais the clock turned to 3.33pm. Immaculate timing. I set the trip meter to zero.

Somehow the speedometer seemed to settle in the groove of 111km per hour. This was a new digital appearance as my previous car was very old and its milometer wasn't digital. In my new car I could watch the constant appearance of the 111 on the brightly lit digital display as I sped down the auto route. This reassured me that the car was in synch with me. All the way down that 111 kept reminding me that this journey was in Divine alignment, for that is what the number 11:11 does. When it appears it indicates (along with intuition) that you are in alignment with Divine will. I had thought that my work in France was finished so I couldn't understand why the 111 was being so persistent. Maybe there was there more to do.

It was good to get back to the ancient stone house even though my ceiling was laced with fine cobwebs and the weeds in the garden were shoulder high. I hadn't been home since the portal opening 7 months earlier when Kate and I had performed a ceremony to open a portal of light within the convent on the date 11/11/11. Each time I returned to the convent I felt a sense of unease. It was a kind of awe, an awe that verged on fear. I approached with a certain amount of trepidation, not knowing what it was I feared. Maybe it was just the raw power of the place. It was as if the building and the land drew up an energetic drawbridge of protection whilst unoccupied. I always approached with a respectful cautiousness. This was no ordinary building on an ordinary plot of land. This was a deeply sacred plot and I was the Guardian.

As I entered I could hear something scrabbling about in the chimney and there was a large centipede sitting on the wall. There were always centipedes in the house, but at last I had an inside toilet which was a luxury. My home was very unusual as it was a detached house sitting on a large plot of land yet it consisted of only one room with a high basement and an extremely tall roof space. It had once been part of a much larger complex of buildings. It was only detached because the buildings on 2 sides had fallen down. It was incredibly tall, in excess of 11 metres but just 5 metres by 5. In effect, it was a tower.

At last I was able to withdraw from the world and try and digest what had been happening over the preceding months. Within the thick stone walls of my old house I spent my days in silence. I was alone and uninterrupted with no phone, television or passing visitors. Thomas. Thomas Becket. Thomas A. Becket. Saint Thomas. Saint Thomas of Canterbury. Becket. His name was running through my mind like a mantra. At this point I still had no idea why Thomas had connected with me. I started some research on the internet which reminded me that the first known representation of Becket was to be found in Monreale Cathedral in Sicily. I don't know why, but Kate and I hadn't visited Monreale when we went to Sicily. I began to get the feeling that I needed to go to Monreale. I had already felt that a trip to Marsala could be on the cards but I had managed to ignore that prompt as I had not experienced any signs around that thought.

"Give me a sign if you need me to go." I addressed that

statement to the ethers, expecting a response in the form of a tolling bell, a fly through from 3 birds or a message on my mobile whilst secretly hoping that no sign would be given. Then I heard the voice of Becket.

"I have given you my sign, dear child. It is there in the corner of your laptop."

I looked. It was still 13.33. Becket was right. The sign had been given.

"I have registered it," I replied with a slightly sinking feeling. "Leave it with me."

I really didn't want to go back to Sicily so soon, but it was clear, thanks to the numbers that like it or not, I needed to return. Fortunately it didn't feel urgent so I just let things be for the time being.

Suddenly I had a strange urge to swing. It was an overwhelming need within me, to feel my body going to and fro. I had noticed that I was rocking involuntarily whenever I meditated, but I paid no attention to it, assuming it would simply pass. I had a swing in the garden and I spent many hours swinging to and fro, looking at the sky. But when it rained I couldn't swing so I needed one indoors. Firstly, I hung my folded hammock from a hook on the doorframe but that did not give me the long, slow, gentle swing that I was seeking. So I put a hook on the wooden ceiling beam 3 and a half metres from the floor. That was better. It was exactly what I needed. The higher the hook for the swing, the slower I swung. Swinging on my hammock seemed to ease the transition into expanded realms of consciousness and I had many insights whilst I dangled from the high ceiling. I felt like a human pendulum as I swung to and fro. There was no better place to be than in the convent. Knowing that nobody could disturb me either by telephone or by knocking on the door (it was unreachable when the garden gates were locked) I could relax into deeper and deeper states of being. In those deep states, three-dimensional time had no meaning and the days passed in a blur. I was Hilary, the neighbour, the human, the daughter of my parents, the mother of my daughter, sister to my siblings and a friend to my friends. I was Hari, a spiritual being on planet earth. But I was also Cynkarta, a starry being from Sirius.

After 11 days of seclusion, and dangling in my pendulum, I decided I needed to get out and about. I was in danger of becoming a hermit. I contacted my friend Glenys and she invited me down to her place for a meal.

"You need to keep on top of your paperwork," she said as she broke a double yolk egg into a bowl to make me an omelette. She looked at it in amazement.

"Strange things always happen when you're around," she muttered, shaking her head.

She broke a second egg into the bowl. That too had a double yolk. She couldn't believe it but I could. It would indeed be wise to keep on top of my paperwork. It was a complete nightmare trying to deal with everything in a foreign language. I needed to get my tax affairs in order so on a beautiful, sunny mid-summer afternoon I set off to the tax office. This being France, the path to the office was picturesque, lined with brilliant yellow flowers whose heads bobbed gently in the soft breeze as I walked past. I entered the completely empty office and pressed the button for a ticket. Ticket number 010. My first thought was that it should have been 111 but at least it was a palindromic binary number. I guess I was only the 10th person to be seen that day.

Despite the fact that I personally thought my spoken French was becoming quite good, as soon as I started explaining my tax situation I was abruptly silenced and told to wait for an interpreter. The interpreter duly arrived, a friendly looking guy with long hair in a ponytail. I recognised him from the night before when I had seen him playing guitar on stage at the night market. It turned out that he was a writer who wrote about signs and symbols. His most recent book was called *Dix tableaux pour domestiquer le buffle.*

"A buffle is a buffalo. The book is a manual of awakening to the realization of unity here and now, in our body, in our present," he explained.

I thought his book was called 'ten tablets of buffalo' because dix is ten and I was under the false impression that that 'tableaux' was French for tablet. (It's not. It's French for pictures. Maybe my French wasn't that good after all!) Mindful of my dream of the young girl on her mother's knee holding a magical tablet that showed all my lives, I googled '10 tablets' and it wasn't long before I came across 'The Emerald Tablet' and what an interesting tablet that turned out to be. Myths tell of a Priest from the long forgotten land of Atlantis founding a colony in ancient Egypt. According to some accounts, this Priest was Hermes Trismegistus also known as Thoth. He was said to be the builder of the Great Pyramid of Giza. He carved some text on an emerald tablet and placed it in the King's Chamber inside the pyramid. The Emerald Tablet is a short text and it said that each sentence related to a mystery or a teaching. I ordered a copy of the translation because I wanted to find out if it had anything to do with past lives. It didn't. But it did mention numbers.

What is below corresponds to what is above, and what is above corresponds to what is below, accomplishing the miracle of the One *Thing. And as all things have come from the* One, *through the* One, *all things follow from this* One *Thing in the same way.*

So that very first sentence contains the number one four times. 1111. Above and below. I filed the information for future use.

At the end of July Kate emailed me a news report dated July 2012. It gave details of widespread corruption and money laundering in the Vatican being revealed again, this time linking the Vatican with Sicilian mafia bosses. I was glad to see darkness coming out into the light of day, especially the link with Sicily. Nothing dark could remain hidden as the earth and her inhabitants move into the higher vibration of Love. That's what lightwork did. It shone light into pockets of darkness.

"For there is nothing hidden that will not be disclosed, and nothing concealed that will not be known or brought out into the open." Luke 8:17

She also sent a picture of 3 black birds, the Coat of Arms of the Becket family. The coat of arms acted as a trigger to remind me once again of Becket. I had switched off from the Becket stuff since I started swinging. I was just enjoying the feeling of being in the body and not in the mind, a human pendulum hanging from the ancient chestnut roof beam. Heading out to the garden to lie and listen to some music, I leaned across the sofa to pick up my iPod. I accidentally leaned on my mobile, which was lying unlocked on the cushion. I heard it bleep as if I had pressed some keys. I had. 2606 was the number that I had not intentionally dialled. 2606. Could that be referring to the 26th June? I looked at my calendar to find out where I had been on June 26th. At Becket's relics...

Chapter 21

Deva Daan

I was working hard on increasing my light quotient, doing lots of kundalini yoga, eating foods rich in prana, lots of mantra chanting...then I had a thought. If everything in the Universe is held in equal balance (like in the yin/yang symbol) then surely by creating more light, I would be creating more darkness too, to keep it all in balance. In a synchronistic twist, one of my Facebook friends (Deva Daan) posted the following:

> *I am currently writing a book and the way I write is, if someone asks something about spirituality the answer comes spontaneously and it surprises both the listener and the speaker. So please feel free to ask me a question.*

I seized this opportunity.

Hilary Question 1: I am increasing my light quotient through certain yoga practises. By doing so, am I creating more darkness?

Deva Reply 1: It depends on how you do the yoga exercises. The yoga exercises are like the foundation of a house. They purify the body so you can proceed with the next step which is meditation.

Meditation is being one with the ocean of consciousness. No technique can lead to this oneness yet a technique can lead us to the point where the jump into the ocean of consciousness is possible. Even watching the mind is a subtle technique. There is duality – there is the watcher of the mind and the mind.

By watching something, we realize we are separate from it. Hence, by watching the mind, we realize we are separate from the mind. When the mind dissolves, we discover our oneness with the universe. There is nothing we can do to attain it. It is simply revealed, spontaneously.

The whole work consists of awakening from the spell of the mind. It is difficult work because the mind has a strong momentum, many lives of constant thinking, thousands of years of thinking.

He had said that the answer would surprise both the listener and speaker and it certainly surprised me because he hadn't answered my question. I tried again.

Hilary question 2: Thank you for your response. I guess what I really am asking about is darkness and light. Is reality light or is reality neither light nor dark?

Deva Reply 2. You suggest that if more light is created somewhere in the Universe, more darkness has to appear somewhere else in order to preserve the "neutrality" of the universal energy…

This is not how the universe works. As far as I see it, everything is light, everything radiates light. When you look at reality without the mind, you see that everything radiates light.

What is darkness? We think of darkness and light as opposites – but they are not. Darkness is an absence of light. If there is no light in the room, it is dark. But we do not know what darkness is. It is a mystery. Because our eyes are trained to perceive things using light, when there is no light, we call this darkness. If we don't see with our eyes, we call it darkness, and we assume there is nothing there.

Darkness is a subjective experience – it is because we look

at reality through a curtain of thoughts – darkness is our inter-
pretation, our dream. Wake up from the dream and see that all
is light.

The mystic does not think, he has no opinions. The mystic
does not interpret reality. So this is our work – to reach a state
of not-knowing.

Reaching a state of not-knowing, our words have power,
and a certain magnetism. Most mystics from India were
uneducated, they practised something simple like a mantra,
and when they woke up they started speaking, but they spoke
from the beyond – their words have a certain magnetism or
power. By removing what you know, space is created in you
so you can truly speak from direct insight.

Deva Daan had translated the works of Ilie Cioara, an
enlightened mystic who lived in Eastern Europe. I googled this
book (*Silence of the Mind*) and I saw the following review:

The poetry here is beautiful: you get a poem, and then an
illuminating prose piece about the poem, lots of each, for 111
pages.

111 pages.

Hilary: Hi Deva, The number 11:11 began appearing in my life
some years ago. It was way, way past coincidence. It was (and
still is) phenomenal. At first it was scary and then I saw it as
magic. As I could not find a satisfactory answer to what it
meant and why it was appearing, I decided I would just
follow it to see what happened. In fact I used the appearance
of this number as a way of living beyond the mind. When I
first emailed you I noticed that the time was 1.11pm. Then I
just went to look at your book reviews for *Silence of the Mind*
and one reviewer mentions the fact that your book has exactly

111 pages. Not many reviews mention the number of pages in the book, so maybe you would like to comment.

Deva: About 11:11, yes, the poem-prose part has 111 pages, and the book was published on 10/11, but the e-book actually came out on 1.11.11.

Everything is connected. Synchronicity is a consequence of the fact that Existence is One. When you are in tune with existence, when you are not lost in the mind, when you are not lost in the constant stream of thoughts and dreams created by the mind, synchronicities happen. Synchronicity is nothing special, it is how this Universe – which is Oneness – works.

Most people are disconnected from the Divine Synchronicity because of the mind. When a human being becomes attuned to Synchronicity, so called miracles will happen. But they are miracles only according to the limited perception of the human mind.

Regarding 11:11. I do not really know if there is a special meaning in this.

If you focus on pigs, you will start seeing pigs everywhere. You will see a pig in logos, on TV, in the newspaper, in unexpected places – and finally, if you focus on it hard enough, you will eventually run over a pig with your car. If you focus on 11:11 you will start to notice it everywhere.

PS: By the way, when I finished answering your question, I looked at the clock on my computer and the time was 11:11

I am not joking. It is true. After I finished your answer, I looked at the clock on my computer. It was 11:11 in the morning.

I laughed. That 11:11 is not subtle. Let's look at the facts. These are physical facts within the physical universe, not beliefs, ideas or feelings. I emailed Deva at 1:11pm, his book has 111 pages, his e-book was released on 1.11.11 and when he finished answering my question he noticed that it was exactly 11:11am. "Welcome to the world of 11:11, Deva," I thought to myself.

Deva says that it is better to perceive the Universe without any thoughts and just be an empty mind. I say: Is the number 11 created by the mind or does it arise from beyond the mind? If we are Universal Oneness then One (1) already exists before mind existed. We can empty our minds and become an empty vessel, which is what Deva was suggesting. We then perceive the Universe without any thoughts. That is what I was trying to do. And that is when the numbers 1, 11, 111 and 11:11 started appearing in front of me, in the physical world.

I didn't agree with Deva's suggestion that it was appearing because I was looking for it. The 11:11 had originally appeared in my life from out of nowhere. I had never heard of the 11:11 phenomenon when it first started happening to me so I had never focussed my attention on it. It clearly didn't come from thought so it could be that the 11:11 comes into the physical universe directly from Oneness (1,1,1,1-ness). If so, why? That is the question I asked when I experienced the 11:11 phenomenon in my own life. When it appeared I by passed the thoughts of the mind and in my quest to find out the reason for 11:11 appearing, I started to make my life decisions based upon its appearance. Could it be that once we are emptied, freed of ego, we can then be programmed by the One Mind? Could 11:11 (a binary number as used in computer programming) appearing in everyday life indicate to us that is what is happening? I believe so.

Chapter 22

The Carer

I woke with a start. I don't know why. One moment I was fast asleep in my bed in the French convent and the next moment I was wide awake. I lay still and listened. It was silent, deathly silent. I glanced at my watch: 03.33am. That's Becket's sign. What's more, I could feel a presence in the room.

"Show yourself," I demanded. "If there is someone there, reveal yourself to me. I am not afraid."

Actually that's not strictly true because I was a bit scared. I'm not quite sure how I would have reacted if a Being of Light, a ghost from centuries ago or Becket himself suddenly materialised in front of me. Despite my demand, nothing appeared so I got out of bed and took a few photos of the room. The flash lit up the dark corners and the spaces between the ancient wooden beams. When I looked at the photos I saw the orbs. There were lots of them, not just one.

The following night I was again woken by my mobile phone ringing. This time it was 00:03am. By the time I had woken up enough to find the phone I had missed the call. It was from 'no number'. Again I felt a presence and again I asked to see who was there. Nobody appeared so again I took photos. This time there were even more orbs. They were under the table, on the walls, up in the wooden beams and one particularly large, bright, brilliant and clear white orb was sitting on my mosquito net. (I slept under a mosquito net as protection from the centipedes.) I was clearly not alone.

Once a week I checked my emails at the local internet cafe. One day there was one from my sister. My mother was ill. She had dementia and had reached the point in her illness where she needed help and support 24 hours a day. She was 89 years old and could no longer care for herself. My sister mentioned getting carers in and even putting her in a home, a thought that was like a dagger in my heart. My mum was born under the sign of Cancer and her own home was everything to her. I looked for number signs on the email to guide me. There weren't any. Date: Sun, 5 Aug 2012, 15:20:53. The time on my laptop was 12:54. Again, no sign.

I didn't know what to do. My home in the beautiful little town of Montignac in France was so far from my mother's home in Somerset, England. It was August and Montignac was in its full glory. The breeze was soft and warm, the sun bright but not unbearably hot, the newly mown hay lay in bales in the fields and swathes of colourful wild flowers decorated the verges. Yet I felt as if I was being called back to England to care for my mother. It wasn't numbers calling me back. It was my heart. My heart took precedence over everything, including signs and synchronicities. I decided I simply couldn't stand by and see Mum put into an old people's home.

If I had no ego I would rush back and welcome the opportunity to serve in this way. After all, as a planetary light server I was on the planet to serve. Yet I literally had to drag myself away from the convent. It was so difficult to exchange my incredible living conditions in France for a cupboard-sized room in my mother's house on a dead end retirement complex. I was concerned at my inability to be filled with joy at the opportunity to serve. Serving humanity when it involved ceremonial work, travelling, group gatherings and celebrations was work I loved. But to be trapped in a location I disliked, cooking, cleaning, bathing, tending wounds and emptying commodes was hard. I was being shown where I still had ego. Ego, ego and more ego. I picked up the photo of Babaji, the immortal Yogi of the Himalayas. I addressed my question to the photo.

"Why is it so difficult? Why am I struggling so much?" I asked.

"Why are you so hard on yourself? Have compassion for the one who is Hilary. She has yielded to leaving France. She is going to care for her mother. Yes she has resistance but she recognises it and doesn't attach to it. She lets it arise, observes it, forgives herself and moves on. Maybe it arises again and again, but with compassion she forgives herself. She knows that she is not these emotions that come and go. She doesn't attach to anything that comes and goes."

"Why is this happening?" I asked.

"I send you every experience to allow you to grow. I am shining the light of awareness into those deep pockets of ego resistance. Once you have looked into those dark corners, they will be dark no more."

I loved the way I was able to have these inner conversations. Whenever I opened up communication with honesty and integrity I was able to receive instantaneous responses from Babaji. Yet I also recognised that Babaji was the pure Divine aspect of which we are all part.

I was then given an image of a plant. Just like a plant is rooted in the earth, so we are rooted in ego, some of us more than others. The image was of this plant being pulled up and the earth shaken off the roots. At first the earth shakes off easily, but to get rid of the more strongly stuck earth, the plant needs to be knocked against a rock to dislodge those last residues. That is what was happening to me. I was being dashed against the rock so no wonder it hurt. But once the roots were free of earth they were clean and could be replanted anywhere. So once I was completely free of ego, I could be sent anywhere and be used as an instrument of light without resistance. This was part of the process of being re-planted from ego consciousness into the world of cosmic consciousness. All residues of the old soil (consciousness) had to be removed.

That is how once more I found myself in the role of carer. This was not the first time I had been put in this role. I had acted as carer to my friend Catherine when we had travelled to India together. It was clear that this was a role that I needed to embrace and not resist; otherwise I knew it would come up again and again. I found myself testing my mother's bath water in the same way that one would for a baby, chopping up her food as I used to do for my toddler, dressing her, putting her shoes on, washing her hair and taking care of all of her personal needs. I was being given the most menial of tasks to teach me humility. I knew I would be kept in the role until I was humble enough. There is no place for pride on the path of number.

I chanted as I bathed her aged body in warm water. I chanted as I shampooed her thin hair. I chanted as I carefully rubbed cream into her bony back. I knelt down and started rubbing the cream into her 89-year-old legs. The skin was paper-thin and I could clearly feel the bones as she had no flesh. She was covered in dark crimson bruises from the blood thinning medication she was taken. The skin felt rough. Gently I rubbed the lotion in being careful not to dislodge the scab that had formed after one of her recent falls. As I knelt at my mother's feet rubbing in the cream, the bracelet on my wrist slipped down onto my hand. It was an Indian bracelet inscribed with the mantra the 'Om Namah Shiva' which is Babaji's mantra. He was reminding me of his Divine presence. He had brought me to my knees, quite literally. Images filled my mind of Mary Magdalene washing the feet of Jesus and of devotees touching the feet of their masters. Deeper and deeper surrender, more and more humility, this is clearly what I was being taught. I had a dream.

I was with mum and we were looking at the sky. I saw what I thought was a comet but I wasn't sure. It could have been a bomb or a weapon. We watched it zoom through the sky, then suddenly it burst in the same way that a firework bursts and lots of silver sparkly heart shapes appeared and gently fell to earth like sparkling snowflakes.

What a beautiful dream that was.

Chapter 23

Fibonacci Numbers

I was exhausted. It wasn't just the fact that I was spending most of the week looking after an 89-year-old dementia patient. Mum's nocturnal cat woke me several times each night by scratching at the door to be let in and out as there was no cat flap. Between the cat and my mother I was lucky to get more than a couple of hours of undisturbed sleep. Then there was the 100 mile commute between my recently built house in Devon and my mother's home in Bristol. I was sleeping on the floor of the only carpeted room in the new place as I had no furniture. Sometimes I was so tired that I knew it would be too dangerous to drive in case I nodded off at the wheel. On those occasions I left my car at my mum's and took the train back. Once I was home I normally spent most of the time catching up on sleep in an attempt to recharge myself for the next nursing shift. I was suffering from a sore throat and I felt seriously under the weather.

28/08/2012. A channelling

It feels like chaos but it's not. It only looks so from your limited perspective. There is a big picture and the wheels move more slowly than your human physical form would like them to. We have it all in hand. Your future home is one that you will love. We have already hinted that that is so. You need not worry. You really are on track and we are guiding you. Do you know anyone else who is being guided as clearly as you? Your task of nursing will be shorter than you imagine. We know it's challenging for you but that is often the nature of growth. The more challenging a situation, the greater the opportunity for growth.

It did feel as if my life was in chaos and it was at difficult times like this that my faith in the path of number could waver. After all, if I hadn't started following numbers then I would probably be living a much less challenging life. I immediately dismissed that thought as a 'what-if" thought, which I try not to allow into my mind. Then, like an unseen hand that was there to help me, someone posted this on my Facebook wall.

"Never doubt My love, not even when I send you challenges and tests, both inside you and in the outside world because everything is for your highest good and for your inner growth." Babaji

My difficult situation was for my Highest Good. I knew that deep down. I also knew that this was how the path of numbers operated. The path of number led me into situations that were for my highest good and through the challenges and lessons I encountered I was led into deeper and deeper states of surrender. It was only my small ego self that wavered when it didn't 'like' a situation, but my faith in numbers never wavered for long as they appeared so frequently and dramatically that I was regularly taken aback by their magic.

The relationship that I have with numbers is now so ingrained into my life that I cannot imagine life without them as my companion and guide. There can be no going back to 'normal' for me. Somehow my life has taken me on this strange and unique path.

Numbers first appeared to me after I began doing Tai Chi and meditation and when I started exploring the non-physical world through energy healing. Number 23 was the first number that appeared. I'm not the only person to have been at the receiving end of a 23 onslaught. The '23 Enigma' even has its own page on Wikipedia these days because it appears in the lives of many people. When it first appeared in my life it was in the days before the internet. In numerology the number 23 is linked to breakdown/breakthrough. With no information on the 23 enigma available and nobody to share my unprecedented experiences with, I really did come close to a 23 breakdown.

The numbers that seem to be the most significant and that appear to me the most often are those numbers at the start of the Fibonacci sequence, namely 0, 1, 2 and 3. The first two numbers in the Fibonacci sequence are 0 and 1, and each subsequent number is the sum of the previous two. The Fibonacci sequence is: 0,1,1,2,3,5,8,13,21,34,55,89,144 and so on.

I knew that the Fibonnaci series of numbers was the under-lying maths of the spiral. I'd looked at Fibonnaci many times trying to find answers to the 11:11 but I had not found the break-through that I had hoped for.

Let's look more closely at this series of number and how they work. I'll start at 144 to demonstrate some facts, though you can start at any number within the Fibonacci series if you wish. The following pattern still works–

144 divided by 89 (the number before it) equals 1.61797752809

89 divided by 55 (the number before it) equals 1.61818181818

55 divided by 34 (the number before it) equals 1.61764705882

34 divided by 21(the number before it) equals 1.61904761905

21 divided by 13 (the number before it) equals 1.61538461538

13 divided by 8 (the number before it) equals 1.625

8 divided by 5 (the number before it) equals 1.6

5 divided by 3 (the number before it) equals 1.6666666666

3 divided by 2 (the number before it) equals 1.5

2 divided by 1(the number before it) equals 2

1 divided by 1 (the number before it) equals 1

So it can clearly be seen that until we reach 3 divided by 2 (in descending order), all the answers begin with 1.6. And after 13th this number is fixed at 1.618 which is known as the golden ratio. Only 0, 1, 2 and 3 do not follow this pattern. Those just happen to be the numbers that had been appearing so frequently in my everyday life.

Geometry and number underlie the physical universe. Really, everything is formed from numbers. Having descended into matter so deeply and having reached that point that is so far removed from our true nature, which is the pure light of love, could numbers be the map that shows us the way back home to source? Our highest nature is a consciousness that is pure love. As a soul on a spiritual journey I have decided to return to source energy so, rather like a knitted jumper being unravelled and being returned to a ball of wool, on my way back to source I am unravelling matter to nearer its true source, which, in the physical universe, is number. In particular, the numbers near the beginning of the Fibonacci sequence.

Chapter 24

White Horse

During this time of caring for my mother my attention was drawn to an event that had been posted online. It was at a location not too far away from where I was living.

This is a call for participants to create a sacred flame ceremony on 9/9. The location is the 5000 year old Wayland Smithy longbarrow in Uffington. I will be working with my 19 crystal skulls and medicine wheel. We will send the sacred flames along the ley lines and timelines.

Nearby is Dragon Hill, where the grass no longer grows. It is said that Saint George slayed the dragon on this hill and his fiery breath scorched the ground. Opposite this is the so called chalk horse – who many regard to be a stylized image of the legendary dragon.

Contact me if you wish to be involved. Laura Pocket

I took note of this posting because of the fact that it was to be held on 9/9. Uffington is famous for the white chalk horse, which had been engraved into the landscape during the Bronze Age. The white horse link clinched it for me because I remembered how Kate had suggested that white horses represent bravery. Then there was the connection with Medusa because she was the mother of the white horse called Pegasus. When I realised that my sister would be caring for my mother on September 9th I immediately knew I would be joining Laura. I contacted her and expressed an interest in the event. I was the only person to respond to her posting.

In the days leading up to the 9/9, 4 crop circles appeared in close proximity to this internationally renowned site. I studied them carefully, looking for clues and messages us to guide us.

The first one was a relatively simple formation composed of a wide circular band with a large central circle and four smaller ones in the area between. It appeared on May 19th. I feel this one was a fake.

On August 12th a genuine and complex circle manifested, full of numerical references regarding the number 12. No doubt that is why it appeared on 12th. Its design reminded me of a rose window.

A third one appeared adjacent to Dragon Hill on August 14th and it was a simple circle that depicted a spiralling serpent. To me a serpent represents kundalini energy, a sign of pure power.

The fourth one appeared just a few days before 9/9 and again it was clearly a hoax circle. This circle depicted a woman's name and a question mark as it had been created by a local man as a unique and unusual marriage proposal. The name of his girlfriend and therefore the name that appeared in the circle was LAURA. I thought that was rather neat. My name didn't appear in a crop circle, but attention was drawn to my surname when I booked into my hotel. I had decided to stay overnight in the Uffington area.

"Name?" asked the receptionist as I handed her my reservation form.

"Hilary Carter."

"Oh yes, you're the first to arrive."

The first?" I queried.

"Yes, none of the others have arrived yet."

"What do you mean?" I asked.

"We have 5 Carters booked in for the night so I assumed you were having a family get together."

There were only 15 of us staying in the hotel that night and none of us knew each other. That's a third of the guests with the surname Carter. In fact, that's 33.3 per cent…

9/9 was the windiest day of the year. It was the type of wind that you could lean into with your full body weight and still remain standing. Laura and I battled against the elements as we climbed higher and higher up the hill, so high that we were soon able to look down on the crop circle next to the white horse. We had a clear view of the serpent. Someone had flattened the grass to add a penis and balls to it. Maybe this was symbolic of the masculine trying to make its presence felt. Although this was the first time I had ever met Laura, it was impossible to converse because of the noise of the howling wind. Only three times did it stop blowing. First, when Laura began to tone, second, when I released a black feather, and the third stilling was when I took out my raw sapphire crystal and laid it on the earth. On each of those 3 occasions the wind stopped dead as if it had been switched off. Each time this happened Laura and I looked at each other in silence for a few moments. We understood the response of the wind and on the third stilling we knew the work was done. Although I wasn't aware of it at the time, this work would be continued exactly 3 months and 3 days later on the triple date 12/12/12.

Chapter 25

The Convent of Mercy

I was still under a great deal of stress caring for my mum and my throat was sore. I treated the energy field in the area of my throat with lapis lazuli crystals, but I was in danger of becoming ill with burn out. Then my stomach started playing up. A visit to my acupuncturist confirmed what I had already suspected, that my earth element was totally out of balance. I wasn't surprised.

"You have depleted your earth energy," she explained. "In other words you are worn out. You need to rest."

"I can't rest. I'm taking care of my mother."

"If you don't rest you won't be capable of looking after her. Make whatever changes are necessary to reduce the pressure you are under."

Her words hit home. I realised that it was the travelling on top of the caring that was one stress too many. It would help if I could find a place to stay somewhere closer to my mother. I looked in mum's local paper and saw that there were some rooms available in a characterful detached house in Clevedon, a small town by the coast just a few miles from mum. It was being advertised by an estate agent called Mark Templer, almost a Templar link. I rang to enquire.

"Where is the house?" I asked.

"Marine Hill."

"What number Marine Hill?"

"It has no number."

"Does it have a name?" I asked.

"Yes. It's called the Convent of Mercy."

A convent. Silent bells echoed in my head when she said that.

"But it's no longer a convent because the nuns moved out a couple of years ago and the building has been sold to property developers. They're going to convert it into luxury apartments and build some houses on the convent land. In the meantime they're letting rooms out so that squatters don't move into the property."

I knew I had to investigate further because this could be the third convent that I had foreseen. Was it to be an English convent rather than Italian? I felt compelled to make an appointment for the following day. As I pulled up in front of the convent to meet the estate agent there was one vacant parking space. I reversed into it. Just before I turned off the engine I noticed that my trip meter was on 222.2.

The house was a solid, square stone building in the shape of a cube. It had 4 storeys and the vacant room was on the top floor. The vacant room was pink, very pink. I looked out of the huge sash window and noticed that I was directly opposite a Franciscan Friary. As soon as I made a note of that fact, the Friary bell rang 3 times. Then there was a short pause then it rang another 3 times. Once again another pause followed by 3 rings. 3x3.

"Thanks," I said to the bells with an inner smile. I love my way of living.

I took the room without hesitation because of the 222.2 and the bells. A week later, when I arrived with my belongings ready to move in, the trip was on 333.3. That was my confirmation sign. I had been guided very clearly to the convent by the number signs and my ego Self had offered no resistance.

And so it was that I found myself living in a community of 15 strangers whose lives had led them towards the former Convent of Mercy. To find myself sharing everything except a bedroom was a shock to the system and it required a huge adjustment on my part. I had to develop tolerance with the 'stud' in the room next door, who kept me awake all night each time a girlfriend stayed over; respect for the woman who took on the task of keeping the stairs and hallway clean; and gratitude for the man who freely shared his internet access with everyone and serenity whilst flushing away someone else's floating turd from the communal toilet. I tried to learn to appreciate the heavy metal music played by the budding heavy metal rock star whose room was next to mine. Each night after work he would practise his singing, screeching loudly along with the thudding music. God knows what the nuns would have thought of it all.

If I thought that my life had already been simplified I was in for a rude awakening as my world was now pared down to one small unfurnished room. I borrowed a mattress to sleep on. I had one pan, one cup, one plate and a knife and fork. I shared the kitchen so I had one shelf in the fridge and one small cupboard space for my food. My clothes fitted into a small basket and my footwear consisted of one pair each of sandals, shoes and walking boots. Yet I didn't feel any sense of lack. On the contrary, I had a feeling of lightness and freedom. It was liberating. Life was so much simpler. I never lost anything for there was nothing for me to lose. Of course I still had a few possessions in my one roomed dwelling in France, but compared to what I had once owned in the way of 'stuff', I now had very little.

The town of Clevedon is situated on the edge of the Bristol Channel, on the shore of an estuary that has the second highest tidal range in the world. Built on 7 hills, the same as Rome, the convent was on high ground and exposed to the elements. The wind whipped through the old house and every morning there was heavy condensation inside the single glazed windows. There was no modern insulation, and although there was central heating, most of the heat quickly escaped through the cracks in the wooden doors and windows. Thieves had stripped the lead from the original roof so there were damp patches here and there, including one on my ceiling.

The house had been built as a hotel, but towards the end of the 19th-century a French order of nuns arrived from France and established a school called St Gabriel's which was in existence until 1912 when the nuns left. After the nuns left the convent lost its name. During World War 1 it was occupied by soldiers. It was in turn a cafe, boarding house and hotel, until 1936 when the Sisters of Mercy arrived. The convent then became known as The Convent of Mercy. It was part of the Mercedarian Order that was founded by St Peter Nolasco after he saw an apparition of the Virgin Mary in 1218.

The nuns started a primary school called St Anthony's which existed until 1991. It was strange how I kept finding myself living in religious teaching institutions, first in Spain, then in France and now in England. This was definitely a repeating theme in my life.

The first convent to appear in my life was a former Franciscan friary in the Andalusian mountains of Spain that I had established in a previous life. I had been killed during the Moorish uprising in 1568. During my time in Spain I was told that an authenticated miracle had taken place within the walls of the friary. Despite comprehensive research, I had never managed to discover the nature of this miracle. Eventually I had given up searching and had released myself from the attachment to the need to know. However, as I now found myself directly opposite a modern day Franciscan friary, I decided that was a synchronicity that I could not ignore. I went to enquire whether any of the brothers had access to some sort of 'dictionary of miracles' that would list my miracle and satisfy my curiosity. The secretary was welcoming and helpful when I explained my mission. Like me she was a Geordie having been born in Newcastle upon Tyne.

"If anyone knows, it would be Patrick. He's a member of the congregation here but he has a lot of knowledge. He has studied Franciscan history in depth. I'll introduce you."

She led me through the red carpeted corridors to the church and introduced me to the man in question. He was dark haired, dark skinned and quite slight, half Italian. His eyes were kind and intelligent. He greeted me with a smile. I duly explained what I was searching for.

"You probably won't have heard of my convent because it's in a rather obscure small Spanish town called Ugijar up in the mountains of Andalusia."

"Oh yes, Ugijar. I know it well. I often spent time in the Alpujarra mountains as my friend had an apartment in that area of Spain. You want to know about the miracle?" he asked.

"Yes, I know that an authenticated miracle took place in the old Franciscan convent that I once owned, but I have never been able to find out exactly what that miracle was. I have even written to the headquarters of the Franciscan order, but nobody could help me."

"It was an apparition of Our Lady. Of course you do realise that the Madonna in the church in Ugijar was a Black Madonna don't you?"

"No I didn't know that."

"She's a very dark Madonna. Her name is La Virgen del Martirio and she's the patron saint of the Alpujarras, not just saint of the town of Ugijar."

An apparition in my convent? I was stunned. Not only that, I could remember how the local saint had made her presence felt within days of my arrival in Spain in 2004. I had arrived in the town of Ugijar in time for the fiesta and I had stood on the convent balcony to watch the procession pass by.

When they reached the convent the entire procession came to a halt. Standing at first floor level on my balcony I was at exactly the same level as Marterio. There I was standing eye to eye with an effigy of a saint, intoxicated by the incense wafting up from the incense burner. I felt as though I was being given a personal message. There was a pause. The band had stopped playing and in that pause, in that sacred space, as I stood alone in the convent, it is as if time was suspended. In that pause, that pivotal moment, I realized beyond

any doubt that there was something very strange going on here. I
didn't yet know what but it was something supernatural.
– *The 11:11 Code* by Hilary H Carter

What I had assumed to be an effigy of a saint was actually a
Black Madonna. She had literally put herself in my face, but I
hadn't recognised her for who she was. For almost 10 years I had
been unaware that she had first entered my life at that moment.
I wanted to know more. As Patrick had a PhD in The Black
Madonna I was keen to pick his brain. I asked about the black
crucifix in Lamezia Terme that I hadn't found and the Black
Madonna in Pizzo, which I came across 'by accident'. Although
Patrick was very knowledgeable he hadn't heard of either of
them.

Some people believe that the Black Madonna represents an
aspect of the Egyptian Goddess Isis, along with Mother Mary
and Mary Magdalene. There is also a strong link between the
Black Madonna and the Knights Templars. Maybe the link goes
back to the black stone that was worshipped by the cult of
Cybele. This stone was thought to have been a meteorite that had
hurtled to earth at the beginning of time.

Chapter 26

The Shrine

It was a cold, drizzly late October day with a cruel, biting wind just to add to my misery. I hated English winters. I longed to be somewhere warm and sunny. I observed that thought arise and as soon as I recognised it as an ego thought form, I let it go. I gathered my bags of shopping and clothes and headed up towards the convent from the car park. I tried taking a short cut through the garden. The grassy bank was steep and my bags were heavy so momentarily I plonked them down on the grass. It was then that I glimpsed something through the undergrowth. It was a beautiful large conch shell sitting on a slab of stone. I carefully parted the undergrowth to reach it and then, to my surprise and delight I saw a stone arch. Within the arch was a painted sculpture of Mother Mary. A shrine!

I picked up the shell and tried to blow it, but it wouldn't sound as I lacked the expertise to play it. I replaced it and returned to my room. In the communal kitchen I noticed a small gold bell on the mantelpiece, cast in the shape of a woman wearing a long flowing dress. I rang it. It had a sweet, soft, feminine sound. Maybe it had belonged to the Mother Superior.

I had been working with the Divine Feminine for many years and now it seemed as if Divine Mother was revealing herself to me in my time of need. There I was, right opposite the Catholic church and Franciscan friary where Mass was held every day, yet I couldn't bring myself to go and attend. That was partly because I wasn't a Catholic but mainly because I was concerned that in fact the Mass that was being celebrated was a black Mass. Pope Benedict VXI was using a twisted crucifix, which had links to black magic. And the Vatican was dark. But I reminded myself that I had webbed the Vatican in geometric light. Maybe I needed to put my human judgements to one side and just go to Mass. When that thought arose I allowed myself to be open to that possibility. So a few days later I slipped in through the back door and sat down to observe Mass. Patrick was there, sitting in the back row. The service was boring so I used the time to read through the history leaflet and learned that the church was 125 years old. Hidden below the altar there were relics of St Francis (the founder of the Franciscans), St Bonaventure, St Antony of Padua, and 4 early Christian martyrs who had been interred in the catacombs in Rome. I spent the rest of the service sending light towards the Vatican. Afterwards Patrick approached me.

"I've got something for you," he said as he pulled a plastic bag from his rucksack. "Some photos. I've been carrying them around for days waiting to bump into you again."

He handed me a folder containing 3 photos. The first one was an exterior view of the Spanish Catholic church in Ugijar that had once been a mosque. A tunnel had connected the church to my Spanish convent. The second one was a picture of the local saint 'La Morenita' which was kept inside the church. She had a very dark brown face as she was a Black Madonna. The third and final one was a picture of an old painting that hung inside the church. This painting also showed the doorway to part of the Spanish convent I had once owned. More disturbingly, it depicted me and my Franciscan brothers being tortured. There were men being hung upside down over vats of boiling oil and suffering other indescribable acts of cruelty. Patrick had no idea that he had handed me a picture of me in a previous life. I didn't say anything. Maybe I would tell him later.

"Did you discover anything else about the miracle?" I asked.

"Yes, the apparition appeared at your Franciscan friary just after the massacre of more than 200 Christians during the Morisco uprising of 1569."

I had been one of those Christians. I had been tortured and beheaded in that life.

"We must meet for coffee," I said. "Then we will have time to talk in depth."

"Yes, as soon as I have a few days off work we will. In the meantime get hold of the book I have suggested," he replied, pointing to some writing on the back of the folder. "It's worth reading. You'll learn a lot from it. I just hope it's not out of print."

I read what he had written: *The Cult of the Black Virgin* by Ean Begg. I ordered a copy online.

I returned to the convent, carefully climbing the slippery wide stone steps to the entrance, wet from the rain. I carefully unlocked the heavy 200-year-old door and turned the large brass handle. Set into the wood of the door was a metal grill at face height that could be slid open, which would have enabled the nuns to see who was at the door without having to open it. A second inner door opened to reveal the large hallway and the sweeping staircase. The ceilings were high but not heavily decorative. There was definitely a sense of austerity within the building, austere yet spacious and welcoming. I felt privileged to be living in such a place and I was beginning to see why I had been guided to this particular spot on the planet. Meeting Patrick was presenting me with a wealth of useful information.

Facebook was particularly helpful to me at this difficult time as I gradually surrendered to my role as carer. Inspirational postings seemed to be aimed directly at me. Sayings such as,

Warriors are not what you think of as warriors. The warrior is not someone who fights because no one has the right to take another life. The warrior for us is the one who sacrifices himself for the good of others. His task is to take care of the elderly, the defenceless and those who cannot provide for themselves.

– Sitting Bull

and

Instead of resenting your experience of the present moment, accept it the way it is. I call it: dropping all unnecessary baggage (irritation, anger, complaining, being the victim...). There is then a beauty and aliveness to each moment.

> The good deepens, the unpleasant dissolves more quickly, and any action you take is more effective. And above all, there is a background of inner peace to whatever you are experiencing.
> – Eckhart Tolle

But the role of carer was still proving very difficult. I (Hilary, my small ego-self) had planned to be in Cambodia for the winter of 2012. I wanted to visit the temples of Angkor Watt on 21.12.2012. In particular, I felt very drawn to the temple that has been nicknamed the 'Angelina Jolie Temple' because it featured in the film *Lara Croft: Tomb Raider*. I certainly didn't intend spending 21.12.2012 in Summerlands. Nobody ever left the Summerlands cul de sac alive. This was a valley of death, a road where people came to live out the final days of their lives. It was so unnatural. It was also very depressing. The sheer heat of the house, the smell, the television and the location were challenging. I wasn't a natural carer. I was a natural traveller, a free spirit who was always happier on the road or sitting in foreign climes.

I could see what was happening. To truly be a conduit of light that could be used to manifest the Divine Plan on earth required all traces of 'Hilary' to be erased. I could no longer attach to that false ego part of me. I had to be in total surrender to where I was led. 'Being a free spirit' was part of my personality. It was an attachment to being Hilary.

However, even though I was living the life of a carer the signs were still coming in thick and fast. A global sign appeared in the form of a magnitude 5 earthquake. It struck just north of Lamezia Cosenza in southern Italy. The quake hit exactly 222 days after

Kate and I had stood outside the locked cathedral in Lamezia Terme and drawn down the light. Because of the 222 connection I was in no doubt that this was the rope of darkness loosening and what a loosening. This quake was felt all the way from Sicily to Molise. It happened at 3.15am. 3/15 is March 15th, the Ides of March and the 315th day of the year is 11/11. I silently acknowledged and understood the significance of the time.

I was allowing myself to let go of everything and become like a piece of driftwood on the tide, allowing the signs to lead me to where I needed to be. My copy of *The Cult of the Black Virgin* arrived and I turned straight to the index. There were only 5 things listed under the letter 'U': Urbicus, Urfe, Uranus, Uriah and Uffington.

Uffington. The White Horse of the 9/9 ceremony. I turned to the relevant chapter and began to read. It started off with details of Epona. That name rang a bell. I glanced down at the clock in the corner of my laptop at the very moment that the time changed from 11:10 to 11:11. That indicated to me that this was obviously of deep significance.

> Best seen from the air, the remarkable stylized horse drawn with white chalk is believed to represent Epona, the Celtic horse goddess. The 374 foot drawing was the focus of ancient religious celebrations. Every seven years, the horse drawing was ritually cleansed.
> Article Source: http://EzineArticles.com/622919

Epona was an ancient Goddess, an early representation of the Divine Feminine. She had powerful connections with the underworld. She was known as a Goddess of fertility and bore the title of 'Great Queen.' How wonderful to see the Great Queen carved into the very earth itself in the form of a white horse.

Chapter 27

The Tanit Cave

The date 11/11/12 was approaching. I rang Kate to ask her where she intended being on that day. My sister was going to be caring for my mother for a week to give me a much needed break so I would be free to go anywhere at all.

"Where are you going to be?" I asked. "It'll be the last 11/11 before the ending of the Mayan calendar."

"I don't know yet," replied Kate. "I guess I'm waiting for some guidance. What about you?"

"I'm off to Ibiza. My friend Jasmine has moved out to a place called Santa Eulalia and I just have such a strong feeling that I need to be there on 11/11. Don't ask me why. I'm just following my intuition."

This happens sometimes. My intuition is very strong, and when I follow it, the numbers soon appear to support me and to validate any actions taken. Kate offered to be involved in any light work that needed doing. She had been involved in the opening of a portal in France on the date 11/11/11. Without her help it wouldn't have been possible. Portals of energy are being opened all over the world. They can't yet be seen by physical eyes as they are made of energy, but they are being put in place in order to establish the new earth. I said I'd let Kate know if I had any signs indicating that she was needed. She let me know that she would be remaining in Canterbury and would help me from her base there.

I wasn't sure why I needed to go to Ibiza. As the Goddess energy was coming in strongly I thought it might have something to do with that. But a niggling voice in my head asked me to remember Turin. I checked the miles as the crow flies —

Santa Eulalia to Turin: 525 miles.

Canterbury to Turin: 525 miles.

I drew the sacred geometry that linked the 3 locations. The angle of the triangle coming out of Turin was 111 degrees. So it looked like Kate did indeed have a part to play and her part was in Canterbury. I had no idea why or exactly where I was needed on the island of Ibiza, but I surrendered to the signs and booked my flights. Shortly after booking the flights online, an advert for accommodation in Ibiza popped up in corner of my laptop. I clicked on it and there was the answer.

The shrine for the goddess Tanit is located in a cave at Es Culleram. You can still visit the cave today. Tanit is the goddess of fertility and that is why a lot of people claim that Ibiza has a feminine energy.

And so it was that on 11th November 2012, exactly 40 days before the famous date of 21/12/2012 I found myself heading for Tanit's cave. When I looked back I saw exactly how I had needed to do nothing for the right people to help me to find the cave had been put into my path. It was Jasmine's neighbour Christine who knew the exact whereabouts of the cave and thank goodness she did for it was well hidden. She had a car, a day off work (11/11/11 was a Sunday) and she wanted to join us for the ceremony.

On the way to the cave we were chatting about numbers in general. Christina asked how I had become so interested in numbers. I explained that it was the number 23 that first woke me up to the strange world of number signs. Following a car accident some years earlier I went on holiday to recuperate. There I met a man who told me about the number 23.

"Just register this. 23 has meaning," he had said, his beautiful bright blue eyes burning into mine.

Arriving back in England after my holiday I experienced the 23 onslaught. Everything in my life was connected to either the number 23 or the reversed number 32. What was strange was the fact that these 23s had existed in my life *before* my holiday but I had not noticed them.

(See *Numerology Made Easy* by Hilary H Carter for the full story.)

I suddenly realised that I had been told about the number 23 in Ibiza because that is where I had gone on holiday all those years ago.

The path up to the Tanit cave was steep but the three of us walked with awareness. Christine found a 2 euro coin and a pink quartz crystal on the way up, good signs as the coin signified abundance and the quartz epitomized the vibration of love. Just as the 3 of us reached the cave, we saw a family arriving from above to join us. It was excellent timing as it was exactly 11:10. We were literally just in time. The family was Domenico, his partner Mary and their 2 daughters.

The weather was beautiful, mild and sunny and everything was unfolding perfectly. The cave was full of offerings to Tanit. Candles, flowers, photos, letters, crystals and all manner of gifts had been carefully placed in and around the cave. Tanit was clearly still worshipped by those in the know.

The rebalancing of the feminine portal at the cave did not take long. All the preparatory work had been done in the preceding months. All I needed to do was to facilitate the spiralling of the energy. The feminine energy was raring to go. It was like a dam bursting open. I knew that Kate was linking with me from her base in Canterbury and I'm sure that's partly why the energy release was so swift. During the proceedings I had linked into the energy of Babaji.

Domenico asked me which Babaji I had connected with because the term Babaji is a fairly generic term that means 'revered father'.

"Haidakan Babaji," I replied. "Have you heard of him?"

"Sure," he replied. "I have spent a lot of time at the Babaji ashram."

"In India?" I asked.

"No, in Italy. It's a beautiful place. It's built in exactly the same way as the main ashram in India, in Haidakan. It's near Bari," he replied.

Bari... connected to Babaji. I was stunned to discover that he had an ashram there and it was good to make a connection with Babaji through this meeting.

Within an hour of the opening ceremony at the cave the storms began. As we drove home the skies blackened and it started to rain. The rain became torrential and was soon joined by a violent wind. The storms that followed the opening of the feminine portal were the worst that had been seen on the island for decades. When the hail finally stopped some 24 hours later, Jasmine and I took a walk along the seafront. The fields and beachfront bars were all ruined. Everyone was talking about the weather. I was saying nothing. Massive storms after a clearing or an opening were becoming a familiar phenomenon to me. I knew this was a cleansing.

The bad weather continued on and off for days. Jasmine and I were stuck in her apartment a lot of the time so I used the time to look on the internet for an event to attend on 21 December. I had planned to be at a small gathering at Andrew's old priory site in Kewstoke in the evening, but for the exact time of the great alignment (11:11am on 21/12/2012) I needed to be somewhere near my mum's house as I would be back in my role as carer by then. Mum couldn't be left alone for more than an hour or two as she was prone to go walkabout.

Although there were ceremonies planned for Avebury and Stonehenge stone circles, I really wanted to attend an event at my nearest stone circle in Somerset, the one at Stanton Drew. The village of Stanton Drew is home to the second largest collection of standing stones in England. However, it soon became clear that nothing had been planned for that site. It was then that I realised. Nothing had been planned because it was up to me to do the required work on that particular stone circle. It was my task. Like it or not, I was the one responsible for the balancing and reopening of the feminine energy for the grounding of the cosmic forces at that site on the pivotal day of 21/12/2012.

Chapter 28

Stanton Drew Stone Circle

Following my trip to Ibiza I finally managed to find time to go in search of Patrick in order to pick his brilliant brain. I headed for the back door of the church, intending to catch him on his way out. Surprisingly, the place was packed with people, unlike the last time when there had only been half a dozen people there. I couldn't see Patrick so I entered and sat down in a side aisle. It was only then I realised that I was at a funeral.

"We are here," began the priest, "to celebrate the life of our dear brother Patrick."

I felt my heart drop. Surely Patrick couldn't have died. But maybe it was a different Patrick. It's a common enough name. Then a man stood up to give the eulogy. It was the dead Patrick's brother.

"How he loved his football team in Liverpool," he said. "As youngsters we always went to matches together."

Oh no. Patrick was from Liverpool. I was a bit annoyed with myself for not coming to look for him earlier. It could be that I had missed a rare opportunity to pick the brain of a Black Madonna expert. I tend to seize the day but it seemed as if I had let this one slip through my fingers. There was so much I wanted to ask Patrick, especially as he was familiar with the town of Ugijar and my first convent.

As I sat there surrounded by a sea of black suits and miserable faces, I looked around for something more pleasant for my eyes to feast on. I was sitting directly opposite the beautiful icons that Patrick had painted. He was such a gifted artist, a man with great sensitivity and talent. He told me he had once repainted the Mother Mary statue at the convent shrine, the one that I had found in the undergrowth. Having feasted on the golden icons I next became aware of the stained glass window just above me to my right. It was a tall, narrow window. At the top of the window was a shield with 3 black birds. They looked familiar, exactly the same as the birds above the Becket relics in Canterbury. Then I looked at the rest of the window. It depicted a very tall man. It was Thomas Becket...

What a strange and incredible world I inhabit, full of wonder and synchronistic thrills. The sun shone through the stained glass window, dappling me in coloured light, tempting me outdoors so I left the funeral. I left not knowing whether I had attended Patrick's funeral or not and walked the short distance to the convent. It was gradually dawning on me that the Convent of Mercy was indeed the third convent to make an appearance in my life. No way was I going to find, buy and move into an Italian convent before the ending of the Mayan calendar on 21st December. The link to Italy was the fact that it was Roman Catholic and that the light work I was doing at this time in my life was mostly in Italy. Having realised that I had found the third and final convent I felt very relieved. I was thankful that I wasn't going to have to learn Italian, deal with buying an Italian property with all the legal tangles that might entail, open an Italian bank account and try working out the Italian tax system. I had already done all that in Spain and then again in France and both times it was a nightmare.

The convent was not too far from my older sister's house. She had moved into an apartment within a medieval castle somewhere in Somerset so I entered her new address into my satnav and set off to visit her in her new home. Despite the satnav, I got lost on the way. Suddenly I saw a road sign indicating that I was entering the village of Stanton Drew. I had no idea that my sister was living so close to this site. Stanton Drew's remarkable prehistoric stone circles have not received the same level of interest and exploration as the more famous examples at Avebury and Stonehenge. The lack of visitors and commercial interest have protected their solitude, energy and character. I knew that it had to be protected in that way until 21/12/2012 because this site was probably the most important gateway of Divine Feminine energy in the whole of Britain. It was far more important than Stonehenge. In fact I got the distinct feeling that despite the fact that it was far more famous than Stanton Drew, Stonehenge was merely an anchor for the energy of Stanton Drew.

There are three stone circles at Stanton Drew. The Great Circle, at 113 metres (370 feet) in diameter, is one of the largest in England, much bigger than Stonehenge. 26 of the upright stones survive although it is thought that there may once have been up to 30. The other two circles are smaller. There used to be short avenues of standing stones but most of these stones have fallen. Recent Geophysical work by English Heritage revealed that the original circle consisted of 9 concentric circles. 3x3.

I pulled in to a pub car park to try and work out where I had taken the wrong turn. A notice in the small car park (with space for only 5 cars) said, 'THIS WAY TO THE COVE'. Curious as ever, I followed the sign to a small, grassy field. As I passed through the old wooden gate into the small grassy field, a flock of black birds shot from the trees and began to fly in circles above me. In front of me stood 2 enormous prehistoric stones that looked like the remnants of a stone circle. A third stone lay on the ground between them. I had the same feeling that I experienced when I entered my French convent after being away, a feeling of awe because of the immense power of the energy. The power was held in the magnificent stillness of these ancient stones. Immediately I knew that this was a portal, a doorway.

It was a bright, sunny autumnal day. The brittle leaves still hung to the trees, rustling in the soft breeze. The sky was bright blue and crystal clear. Against that backdrop I could see the squat, square tower of an old English church a short distance away. I leaned against the largest cove stone, my spine in contact with this stone, an ancient part of English history that had stood on this site for thousands of years. The 13th-century church adjacent to the Cove was a mere baby in comparison. I asked for some healing, which I received through the soles of my feet. It felt like an electric charge. My feet began to tingle as if I was standing on vibrating plate. Energized and humbled by the power of this site, I headed towards the main stone circle. I walked along the narrow country lane, past the quaint pub (The Druid Arms) and past the 11:11 war monument. I turned into a cul de sac of modern houses. It seemed quite incongruous to have such buildings adjacent to a truly ancient monument. As I entered the circle it was inevitable. My mobile showed the time – 11:11.

Unlike the famous stone circle at Stonehenge where it is not possible to get anywhere near the stones, Stanton Drew was completely open and accessible. There was no ticket office, simply an old wooden honesty box nailed onto the rickety gate in which to place your £1 donation. There wasn't a soul around, just a whole load of black and white cows. Hundreds of black crows filled the sky, cawing loudly as they flew crazily above my head. I walked carefully across the rough field, treading carefully between the dozens of steaming cow pats. This was a farmer's field and was in regular use by his herds. Stanton Drew stone circle doesn't have the same visual impact as either Stonehenge or Avebury despite the fact that it is larger than Stonehenge. Maybe that's because some of the stones are smaller and more spread out. However, to be able to enter the very centre of the circle and to be able to lean against the stones is something that it is rarely possible to do at Stonehenge. What Stanton Drew lacks in impact it makes up for in raw power. I spent an hour at the stones and not a soul passed by. I could have stayed there all day, but I was already running late so I vowed to return as soon as possible. However, despite the fact that I was short of time I simply couldn't resist calling in at the adjacent church on my way back to the car. I have a deep attraction to old ecclesiastical buildings. This particular church is dedicated to St Mary the Virgin. There was a bible on the pulpit. When I find an open bible in a church I always look for the message that awaits me on that page. When I find a closed bible, I open it at random. This particular bible was closed but there was a large bookmark of red ribbon attached to the spine. What message was contained on the page that was marked by the red ribbon? The book was very old and fragile, quite large and heavy and beautifully bound in leather, so I used both hands to carefully open it. I gasped in delight because it was marking page 1111. My whole body was in wonder at this amazing synch. I could feel the magic in my very cells.

Page 1111. Ephesians, the 10th book of the New Testament. Chapter 5. Naturally I scanned down to verse 11.

[11]Have nothing to do with the fruitless deeds of darkness, but rather expose them. [12]It is shameful even to mention what the disobedient do in secret. [13]But everything exposed by the light becomes visible—and everything that is illuminated becomes a light. [14] This is why it is said:

"Wake up, sleeper,
rise from the dead,
and Christ will shine on you."

Chapter 29

Tesla

I had never met Edward. He was a member of the White Eagle Lodge and had emailed me as he wanted to open up a discussion on spiritual matters. He lived in the Isle of Man, a small island off the coast of England with less than 90,000 residents. One day I was musing on Medusa and the strange 3-legged symbol on the flag of Sicily. I found out that it only appeared on 2 flags in the world; Sicily and the Isle of Man.

> Hi Ed, now here's an odd synch that links with you... I have been trying to find out why Medusa has been appearing in my life and I looked at the flag of Sicily. The flag of Sicily is very unusual as it depicts Medusa with 3 legs coming out of her head. The only other flag that contains the image of these 3 legs (known as a triskelion) is the flag of the Isle of Man...Love, Hx

> Hi Hilary, for me the number 3 symbolises the sacred triangle. I have recently felt the power of the holy trinity through visualising the triangle – divine father, divine mother and the son (the Christ). Perfectly balanced and bringing harmony. The 3 legs of the triskelion are also representative of perfect balance. The number 3 is also very important in the White Eagle Lodge – the hours of 3, 6 and 9 are meant to be very sacred and very good times for sending out the light and healing to where it is needed. However, I have also recently been given the number 7 as being a key. Love from Ed.

Many people like the number 7 and consider it to be lucky but it hadn't made much of an appearance in my life. For me the numbers 0, 1, 2 and 3 continued to be the most prominent with the 11:11 and 333 seemingly carrying the most power. Ed's mention of 3, 6 and 9 was relevant because those are the numbers that Nikola Tesla was obsessed with. Tesla was an inventor, electrical engineer, mechanical engineer, physicist, and futurist. He once said, "If you only knew the magnificence of the 3, 6 and 9, then you would have a key to the universe." Tesla became obsessed with the number 3. "...he often felt compelled to walk around a block three times before entering a building, and demanded 18 napkins (a number divisible by three) to polish his silver and glasses and plates until they were impeccable whenever he went dining." (Amy Mast. America's forgotten innovator, Nikola Tesla (PDF). Florida State University. pp. 14–15)

It was good to read about another human being who had an obsession with numbers. I would have loved to have joined Tesla at the dinner table to discuss 11:11, 23 and 333. Amongst other things, he invented the induction motor, a death beam that would end war on the planet, and he was working on a method of using earth as a conductor to generate completely free electricity for the entire world. His notes and workbooks were confiscated by the American government after his death. Doubtless worldwide free electricity would not serve the global elite and so his secret died with him, along with his 3/6/9 obsession.

Tesla died in room 3327 of a New York hotel, 6 short of a 3333. 4x3s. I was in room 4D of the convent. D is the 4th letter of the alphabet and therefore 4D is 44, the number of safety and security. I did feel safe and secure but it wasn't easy adapting to communal life in the convent, especially as we were a disparate group of souls without a common purpose or aim, unlike a spiritual community with a joint vision. There were about 15 people living there, people of all ages and both sexes. Some were night workers, others on mixed shifts. People came and went all day and night, banging the doors and waking me from deep, exhausted sleeps. There were a few retired people who were around all day. Some people socialised into the early hours and came in drunk in the middle of the night. Caring was physically, mentally and emotionally demanding work and I needed to catch up on sleep on my days off. My eye had started to twitch involuntarily. To me that was a dangerous sign because I knew from past experience that this only happened when my physical body was under severe stress.

Fortunately I had only taken a 3 month lease on the room in Clevedon. The date was November 19th 2012 and if I intended staying on I needed to let the landlord know. If I was going to leave, I needed to find somewhere else to live. I scoured the internet for houses in the county of Somerset within 40 miles of my mother's house. After my experiences at the convent I didn't want anybody living above or below me so I wasn't searching for an apartment. There were hardly any houses available for my budget. However, I was surprised to see that there was a small one bedroom end of terrace in a place called Watchet available for rent. It was a characterful period property and it immediately caught my eye. I had never visited Watchet and I knew absolutely nothing about the place so I googled it, noticing as I did so that the time was 11:01am.What on earth could Watchet have to do with my number journey? It is a small fairly obscure town situated on the edge of the Bristol Channel. I can honestly say that my mouth fell open in shock when I googled it and read the following:

Man has been in and around Watchet since the dawn of time. An Iron Age fort can be found on the western fringe of the town. The Saxons established a Royal Mint here in the time of Alfred the Great. The Norman families in the area provided two of the Knights who in 1170 were involved in the murder of the Archbishop of Canterbury, Thomas A Becket. To atone for this atrocity the disgraced Knights commissioned the building of Watchet's uniquely named St Decuman's Church. http://www.aboutbritain.com/towns/watchet.asp

I was awe-struck by this connection with Thomas Becket. I live in a world of everyday miracles yet when one like this appears I can still feel astounded. I love my miracles and I certainly don't become complacent or take them for granted. Saint Decuman was a saint I had never heard of. The name is thought to derive from the Latin *decumanus*, which means 'a farmer of tithes' but I prefer the '10' connection as his name could be derived from the Latin *decumanus*, a variant of *decimanus* (of the tenth), from *decimus* (tenth), from *decem* (ten). The word was often applied to waves from the belief that every tenth wave is greater than the others. So, to my way of thinking, the name Decuman had its roots in the number 10.

When I looked up the latitude and longitude I saw that the longitude of the house in question was exactly 3.33. Exactly 3.33, not approximately. What a sign that was. Utterly amazing! At 3.33 longitude and an average elevation of 3 metres there was certainly a strong '3' connection. But I needed more than this to convince me to move there. It was absolutely clear to me that the town of Watchet was being brought to my attention but did I have to go and *live* there? Maybe I could just go and visit? However, as with the number prompt 11:11, other repeated digits such as the 22 and 33 were sent to guide me to overcome the judgements and limitations of the mind and the likes and dislikes of the ego.

I am sometimes asked, "What does the number 444 mean?" or "I looked at the clock at 11:11am. What does that mean?" On their own the numbers are not meaningful. It is when they interact with our consciousness that they can be read as messages. For example, if I was thinking about visiting a friend in Portugal and I noticed that the time was 5:55 then I would see that as a sign to go. If more than one sign appeared around that thought then I would interpret that as the numbers being very keen for me to go, indicating that it would be good for my Higher Self to take the trip. My Higher Self was clearly very keen to send me to Watchet. I was lying on the bed with my eyes closed thinking, "I wonder if I could just visit the town rather than go and live there. It would be so much easier than moving." I opened my eyes and it was 1:11pm. Then later that day I was with my mum and she was watching television. I lay there wondering how many churches in England had been dedicated to Saint Decuman as I had never heard of him. I glanced up just in time to see an advert on television offering a steam cleaner for 3 equal payments of £33.33.

Each sign felt like a nudge in the ribs, a constant nudging that simply couldn't be ignored. At times like this, when the signs appear one on top of another, I know that things are hotting up. I'm being shoved rather than guided in a certain direction. In this case the direction was Watchet. Of course what I wanted was an answer to the question, "What do I have to learn or discover in Watchet?" But I knew that the answer would have to be preceded by a leap of faith, namely signing a rental contract for the house and committing to going to live in a new town. First I needed to view the place. I thought about going to visit the following day, November 20th but the letting agent was busy and couldn't fit me in until November 22nd. That's 22.12.2012. That's a number pattern so I could see that I was being guided. 22nd November is famously the day that President John F. Kennedy was assassinated. It is also the date that C.S. Lewis died.

You don't have a soul. You are a soul. You have a body. C.S. Lewis.

The 22nd November wasn't ideal as I had intended being in Glastonbury Tor for the 11th gate activation. Thousands of light workers all over the world were contributing to this work, the opening of an energetic gateway that would trigger the final clearing of all remaining darkness and duality on planet earth. The opening of these gates was facilitated by a woman called Solara. The work began on January 11th 1992 (11/1/1992) and was a 20 year process of activating 11 gates within the 11:11 doorway (see Solara's website www.NVisible for further details).

If I went to Watchet I wouldn't be able to join a group event in Glastonbury. I looked online to see if there were any 11th gate events in the Watchet area but there weren't. So I looked at the map to see if there were any ancient monuments or megaliths nearby. That's when I found the holy well. St Decuman's Holy Well is in Watchet Somerset. The Well was a sacred site in Celtic times.

That sounded perfect. I would visit the well and go and see the house on November 22nd. That date is written as 22/11 or 11/22. 11 and 22 are the two master numbers in numerology and added together they make 33. The complete date of 22/11/2012 added up to 11 so it was actually a master number day. I asked for a lunchtime appointment to view the house but was told I could either have 3pm or 3.30pm. I could have guessed that would be so.

Chapter 30

The 11th Gate

The 22nd day of the 11th month duly arrived and I was woken early by the sound of gale force winds and rain lashing against the single glazed windows of the convent. The old sash windows rattled violently as if they might burst open at any moment, helpless against the strength of the wind. A storm was sweeping up the Bristol Channel and, being on the 4th floor and near the top of a hill, my room in the convent was particularly exposed to the elements. I looked out of the kitchen window and I could see the storm out at sea. The sky hung black and threatening above the choppy waters like a heavy, dark, oppressive veil.

"There's an amber warning out today," said the news reader on the radio. This warning of difficult driving conditions was followed by a list of roads that had been closed due to flooding. There had been a landslide in a nearby town and the local railway was completely out of action due to flooding on the lines. A man had drowned in the next village after his car was swept away by the storm. Huge potholes had appeared in some roads and trees were falling down all over the place. This was far from perfect driving weather, but I had to go. I was committed to being at the holy well. I would just have to drive carefully. I took the B3133 out of town. From here the journey took me along the M5 motorway. The visibility was dangerously bad. I put my wipers on rapid and kept out of the fast lane. The gale force winds battered my car and I struggled to keep it moving in a straight line. I was glad to turn off the M5 at Bridgwater.

As I drove I was aware that the opening of the 11th gate was a very important occasion for me. That's because the number 11 has played such a huge role in my life. So, on this journey I was highly tuned to signs, much more so than I normally would be. I was utterly and completely in the moment and everything that I encountered in my path I deemed to be significant.

Some of the most significant and helpful number signs appear on my milometer and trip meter. I always put the trip to nought whenever I fill up with petrol and I always note where I am when it reaches 111.1, 222.2 or 333.3. I have never managed to drive 444 miles on a tank of petrol so the trip never reaches 444.4. The milometer is a deeper sign than the trip as it only reaches each number once in its lifetime and it can display all repeated digits from 1 to 9. I would interpret the 11,111.11, 22,222.2, 33,333.3, 44,444.44 and so on as very powerful signs. Occasionally the trip and the milometer synchronise and I am presented with 2 signs at once. This is a 'double prod' from the world of numbers and in my experience, always highly significant. For example, 111,111 on the milometer in conjunction with 33.3 on the trip would alert me to the fact that there was something in my universe at that precise moment that I needed to take note of. All I need to do is to find the message. It could be the words of a song on the radio, a signpost, the place I am driving through at that moment or a thought I am thinking.

As the trip meter in the car reached 2222.2 I noticed a large speed limit sign on either side of the road, indicating that the maximum speed was 30mph. I drove between the 30 and 30 and as I did so I felt as if I was going through a 3030 gateway. A bit further on the trip meter reached 2233.3. At that very moment I was driving over a sign painted on the road said. It said SLOW DOWN. This message was written between 3 unbroken yellow lines, 3 lines above the writing and 3 lines below. I recognised these lines as hexagram 1 from the I Ching, the Chinese book of Changes.

If your goals are in alignment with the greater good, and you assert yourself in a positive way, your actions will meet with success. Call upon creative power and let it work through you. Stay focused on

your goals; do not let yourself be distracted, or you may lose the power available to you now. And remember that when taking action, success requires good timing.
– Hexagram 1

I took heed of the message. I slowed down and I was glad I did because as I turned the next sharp bend I had to swerve to avoid a deep flood that completely blocked my side of the road. Thankfully there wasn't anything coming in the opposite direction or I might not be writing these words today.

I was driving through exceptionally beautiful countryside as I was skimming the edge of the picturesque Quantock hills, an area of outstanding natural beauty. The brutal winds were rapidly stripping the trees of their leaves and whipping twigs and small branches at my windscreen. The nearer I got to the holy well, the worse the weather became. The roads were almost impassable in parts. I continued to drive really slowly and fortunately there was not a lot of traffic around. Most people had wisely heeded the traffic warnings and stayed at home.

As I drove through the dancing leaves I realised that it was exactly 9 years to the day since I had started my 11:11 journey. 3x3. I informed my Divine Self that if she wanted me to move to Watchet then I needed to see the number 33 on this day. I imagined that it would all be down to the milometer. I pulled up outside Saint Decuman's church. The milometer read 2244.3, not highly significant but not totally insignificant either as there were 2 sets of repeated digits and the number 3, Becket's number. A hand written sign directed me to the well. It was down a steep, muddy track below the ancient church. Legend says that the local pagans cut off the saint's head after which St Decuman carried his own head to the well where he washed it, placed it back on his shoulders and carried on with his sacred work. The entrance was through a canopied gate. A hand painted sign saying 'Saint Decuman's Holy Well' was nailed to the canopy. As I stepped over the threshold a particularly strong gust of wind hurled hundreds of leaves from the trees and in an instant I was showered in a generous confetti shower of coloured leaves.

"Oh my God, it's beautiful," I whispered to myself as I stepped through the gate. Despite the weather I could feel the magic of this place. Having been blessed by nature's confetti I made my way carefully down the slippery steps that were thick with fallen leaves. They were carpeted with a layer of bright pink fuchsia flowers that had been freshly dislodged by the wind.

There were quite a few coins in the well for this site was known locally as a sacred place, yet I had never heard of it. It was enclosed within an arched canopy built from rough stones and cement, reminding me of the shrine in the convent garden, womb-like and therefore deeply feminine. Above the arch stood a simple wooden cross. The well was overflowing because of the amount of rain. The water gushed down the hillside into a small pond and from there into yet another, 3 round containers of clear sacred water. A stone sculpture stood in the corner of the garden, engraved with a verse from the book of Genesis: "God breathed and man became a living soul." Genesis 2:7

There are two type of water on earth. There is the water table water, which is rain water that has been absorbed by the earth. Then there is primary water. Primary water is created deep in the earth as the by-product of various chemical reactions. This water is forced up towards the surface of the earth where it emerges as a spring. This type of spring is called a 'blind spring' and they are known to be places of healing. All authentic holy wells are blind springs. In fact you can find primary water under every valid holy site. These springs are normally found on ley lines, which are rivers of energy.

The holy well was beautiful. I stood for a while listening to the sound of the flowing water in the shadow of the tower of the 13th-century church. Then I held my blue sapphire pendulum above the water to see which way the energy was flowing. It began swinging in an anti-clockwise circle, huge circles of movement, completely undisturbed by the wind thanks to the protection of the arched stone canopy. Despite the fact that it had been named after a male saint, this was a Goddess well. My sapphire continued its circular movement. I was totally mesmerised, drawn into the deep, dark depths of that pool of holy water. It felt like the ancient spring in Siracusa, that fathomless eye of water that had looked deeply into my soul. I couldn't take eyes off my sapphire. I was totally engrossed in the movement of the crystal above the water. There was a blurring of boundaries as the pendulum appeared to merge into the womb of the well. I felt as if I was spinning like the sapphire, dissolving into the false constraints of time. Time no longer existed. I was just swirling energy. Round and round went the pendulum. Above the water it appeared bright and clear and solid. Below the water its reflection was faint and shadowy and dark and deep. I lifted it away from the water, still swinging. The pendulum swung anti-clockwise, yet when I lifted it up and away from the water and viewed it from underneath it now appeared to be going clockwise.

That's when I understood.

I had always thought of the pendulum as swinging from right to left like a clock pendulum, but when I noticed the difference in direction when observing the pendulum from below rather than above, a shift occurred. The phrase 'As above, so below' came into my mind, the phrase that I had filed away from the writing on the Emerald Tablet. The pendulum swings in circles or even spirals and the concept of duality that I had been struggling with was not a 'to and fro' duality but an 'above and below' duality. The surface of the water at the point of stillness is zero point. I then had an image of the Fibonacci series of numbers, the numbers behind the created Universe, reflected against itself.

144,89,55,34,21,13,8,5,3,2,1,1,0 ? 0,1,1,2,3,5,8,13,21,34,55,89,144 etc.

Just look at the middle section. 3,2,1,1,00,1,1,2,3. My number journey had begun with the numbers 32 and 23 appearing in my life, followed by number patterns formed from 0s, 1s, 2s and 3s. The 11:11 showed up followed by zero and then the symbol of the eye. It was clear that this was happening as I was coming back to zero point, to that place I had been in before I acquired an ego and therefore separation from Oneness and all that is. I see the numbers as a physical manifestation of movement through gateways of consciousness. As you approach zero point you are coming to the very building blocks of the physical universe. Zero point manifested to me as the all-seeing eye, which is not a number but could be the doorway into the 4th dimension. It is the eye observing itself, the 'watcher and the watched' as Deva Daan had explained.

"Wow," I repeated to myself over and over again. There at the holy well the coin had dropped. It was a very appropriate place for that to happen as the well was a place where people came to drop coins and make a wish. And the town was called Watchet. You can't get much closer to watcher and watched than that. With this revelation in place I picked up my phone. It was 11:33. I had been there for exactly 33 minutes, though it had felt timeless, as though I had been suspended beyond time.

I realised that I had been so engrossed in the swing of the pendulum that I hadn't noticed that I was getting soaked through in the rain so I sought shelter in the church of Saint Decuman, adjacent to the well. The Church is some way out of the centre of Watchet but it is there because of the holy well, which was the place of worship before the coming of the Christian faith. It was, as is usually the case with old English churches, completely empty. I looked for an open bible but there wasn't one. However, there was a small pile of papers on a seat in the choir stall. The Vicar had left his or her sermon behind, so being curious, I read it. It was all about the trinity. The number 3 again. In fact there were exactly 11 pages all about the number 3. In an egoless word, fact really is much stranger than fiction.

The following words are taken from the sermon.

> The word Trinity isn't in the bible as it was a word invented by the early church. In the first verses of Genesis we read of God creating the universe. In revelation we read of God in Jesus as the beginning and the end – the alpha and the omega. And throughout scripture between Genesis and Revelation we read of the relationship between God the father, Jesus the son and God the Holy Spirit.

Becket's remains were kept in Trinity Chapel in Canterbury Cathedral. Maybe it's so called because of his link with the Trinity. According to Wikipedia, Becket was consecrated Archbishop of Canterbury on the Sunday after Whit Sunday, and his first act was to ordain that the day of his consecration should be held as a new festival in honour of the Holy Trinity. This is known as Trinity Sunday. This link between Becket and the number 333, the trinity number appearing in a trinity, confirmed to me that I was in contact with Becket But I couldn't understand why the number 333 was appearing if I had managed to get back to zero point. Was I going backwards in my journey towards source energy?

After reading the sermon I still had a few hours until my 3pm appointment with the estate agent so I called in at the local corner café for a bowl of hot soup and shelter from the dreadful weather. As I entered I couldn't help but notice a large wooden calendar on the counter. In large, red wooden capital letters it stated: '33 DAYS UNTIL XMAS.'

I had asked for a 33 sign. Surely this was it? I had no idea that November 22nd was exactly 33 days until Christmas until I saw that wooden sign. I sat there pondering the fact that it was the 22nd day of the 11th month and it was 33 days until Christmas. As I sat in the warm, steamy café waiting for my soup, I watched the staff decorating the Christmas tree.

"The lights aren't working properly," said the first woman.

"Where is the switch for the lights? Put them off then on again," said the second woman. Once again I remembered Kate's son mentioning a switch for a light.

"It's no good. They're broken. Every 3rd light is out."

The road outside the café was very narrow, barely wide enough for a single vehicle to pass through. That was because there was a stone building just opposite the café window. It was clearly very old as the stone arches above the windows were heavily weathered. It was very difficult for cars to get round the sharp corner but I liked the fact that the old building took precedence over the cars. I asked what it was.

"Oh, that's the museum. Well, it's a museum downstairs, but upstairs is a chapel. It's the Holy Cross Chapel. "

After my late lunch I went in search of the rental house and found it down a narrow lane. It was a tall house half covered in ivy and it looked somewhat neglected. The paint was peeling from the window sills and there were several large cracks in the rendered walls. I stood outside in the pouring rain, trying to protect my ears from the biting wind that was blowing, clutching my multi-coloured scarf to my head with ice cold fingers. This was a particularly harsh winter. How I hated English winters. A man came scurrying up the road battling against the elements, clutching a file, holding it close to his chest so that it would not be blown from his grasp.

"Sorry I'm slightly late," he said.

I glanced at my phone – 3:03. My heart sank slightly because the signs were quite strong. I just hoped that the interior of the house was not as bad as the exterior.

"I'll let us in out of this weather," he said as he struggled to put the key in the lock. As he battled to open the warped wooden front door, I looked around. There was a car parked right outside the house with a very significant number plate: AAA 11 AA. It was one of only 2 cars parked in the road as there were only 4 car parking spaces in the lane. I stared at it in disbelief. That is an indescribably rare number plate.

There was a ceramic plaque on the wall outside indicating that the house was number 4 in the road, the number of safety and security. Number 4. That could represent the 4 knights. The plaque was illustrated with 2 kingfishers. We entered the tiny hallway. The house smelt damp. The steep stairs were directly ahead and the kitchen was on the right. It was basic, uncared for and very, very dated. The oven must have been at least 40 years old. I swear it was exactly the same model that my mum had cooked on when I was a child. The plaster on the wall by the window was uneven. I touched it and a huge chunk fell to the floor with a thud. It was soaking wet. The electricity meter above the door was wrapped in black cobwebs and it was the old-fashioned type of meter with huge pull out fuses. We climbed the dark, winding stairs. There were no windows in the stairwell. The carpet was so thin and worn that I could see the imprint of the floorboards underneath. On the first floor was a tiny bathroom with no shower, just a bath. The soil pipe of the toilet wasn't boxed in and there was black mould growing on the wall. The bedroom was small with 2 single-glazed windows, one looking directly into the house opposite and the other with a view of the road. The walls weren't even plastered. They were lined with hardboard and the wallpaper was peeling in places. A narrow, winding staircase leading to the top floor opened into the largest room where I was stunned to see a completely uninter-rupted view of the 1000-year-old harbour. It had always been my dream to live overlooking a harbour. I stared out at the stormy sea beyond the harbour walls. I couldn't take my eyes away from the incredible view. Imagine what it would be like to be able to see that every day. From the other window I could see the tower of Saint Decuman's church sitting on top of the hill. Again it was an uninterrupted view. This place had such special views but the accommodation was basic to say the least. In fact I would deem it virtually uninhabitable. The house could have been so lovely if it had been cared for properly.

"They're very old windows," I commented as I tried to open one. It was an old wooden window, and like the front door, it was warped with damp. I managed to force it open, and as I did so a shower of large black flies fell from the top of the window. They fell into my hair, over my face and onto my clothes. I screamed.

"Yuk, they're horrible," I cried as I desperately tried to brush them off. There were dozens of them; large, fat, lazy buzzing flies that I later found out were called cluster flies. The estate agent laughed as I danced crazily around the room in a state of distress, throwing my scarf and coat to the floor in an attempt to shake them off. That was a disturbingly bad sign, I thought to myself as I retreated hastily from the room. The contrast between the two showers could hardly have been greater. In the morning an exquisite shower of multi-coloured autumn leaves. In the afternoon a disgusting shower of dead and dying flies. I said that I would let the agent know my thoughts on the house when I had considered it. I left and drove back to the convent through the driving rain. It was then that my mind began the torment.

Chapter 31

Franz Ferdinand

At the beginning of this book I described how the number signs need to be acknowledged, run past the intuition and then acted upon. The block to action is mind interference. It was at this point in my journey that I was reminded of what could happen if I allowed the mind to interfere. I could of course have just immediately have surrendered to the signs without any ego resistance and said, "Yes, I'll rent the house please." The signs had been obvious enough, all those 3s. If I was totally clear of ego and completely surrendered to the signs I would not have hesitated to do that. Instead, I put myself through days of mental anguish. My mind was clearly still in a position to sway me, to interfere with my connection to source energy. I was having a major battle regarding Watchet. I had come quite a long way on my 'undoing the ego' journey but it was clear that I had still had ego and it was being shown to me. I struggled with thoughts of 'what if?' and 'why?' My mind threw up all sorts of obstacles and fears to try to prevent the free flowing of energy that was so clearly guiding me to the quaint little town of Watchet.

"You don't know anybody living in the area."

"It's an isolated place."

"Transport links are virtually prehistoric."

"Face facts-the house is a dump."

"The old electric cooker is prehistoric."

"The carpets had no underlay and they were so worn. How could you live with carpets like that?"

"The damp walls...the black mould..."

"It has no garden. How can you live without a garden?"

"There's no parking. How can you live without parking?"

"Those flies. Yuk! Isn't that a really bad sign?"

"Moving again? Can you handle that? Just imagine the work involved in having to change your address on all of your paperwork and all of your online accounts."

But the still, silent part of me could see what was really happening, namely that I had been given loads of signs and I hadn't acted on them. I reflected on the signs I had been given.

- There was the incredible link with the knights who killed Becket, a major and stunningly magnificent sign that completely blew me away.
- The '33 days to xmas' sign in the café.
- 3.33 longitude (another stunning sign).
- The Trinity sermon (a direct link to Becket).
- The time of the appointment 3pm.
- The arrival of the estate agent at 3:03.
- The fact that every 3rd light on the Christmas tree lights was unlit.
- The comment about the switch in the café.
- The 'AA 11 AAA' number plate of the car parked outside the house.

I thought that the last of those signs was the most curious. A car with that number plate parked right outside the house? It was a one in a million line up of that particular letter/number combination. But still I was hesitant. The milometer had not contained a sign, nor had the trip meter. That was very unusual. Should I take the house or should I stay at the convent? Would it be crazy to act on the signs and move into a dump? Did I need to move or could I just be aware of the existence of Watchet? I was bemused, puzzled, confused. My mind was alive and kicking and it hurt.

The sun had made a rare appearance in the English winter sky so I made the most of it and went for a wander in the convent grounds. I love to walk. It stills the mind and brings me into the moment. The garden was overgrown and the branches stroked my face as I took the steep, overgrown stone path down to the shrine. Maybe being in nature would give me clarity.

"It's so special here," I said silently as I stood looking at the Mother Mary shrine. I tried to imagine the French nuns building this beautiful arch with their own hands long ago in the 1800s. What would happen to it when the convent was redeveloped? I hoped it would stay as it was for not only was it an important part of the history of Clevedon, but it was a focus point for the Divine Feminine energy and a wonderful place to go and find inspiration.

"I'm struggling," I said to Mother Mary. "Please help me with this Watchet decision. I am open to being guided but I need clarity on this issue."

My prayer was a plea for release from the mental turmoil I was experiencing. The mind can be a hard animal to tame. I could see the water of the Bristol Channel from where I stood. Yes, it was a lovely spot yet it did not hold the same magic as the holy well at Watchet. That well was so ancient that it had probably been there since the dawn of time. I placed my bag on the damp stone step and sat on it. It felt good to sit in the winter sunshine. The calm weather was a welcome relief after the ravages of the storm. I sat in stillness with my spine upright and my inner gaze at the point between my eyebrows. I don't know how long I sat there but when I re-opened my eyes they immediately alighted directly on 4 fuchsia flowers. These were the same flowers that I had seen at the holy well. Suddenly Kate's name just dropped into my head, seemingly from nowhere. I had to ring her. I didn't know why. I just had this overwhelming urge to ring her so I did.

"I don't know why I'm ringing you," I said when she picked up. "I just know I have to call you."

"Oh, that's strange. I was going to ring you today," she said in surprise when she heard my voice.

As soon as we started talking I heard the droning of an approaching helicopter. It was circling the sky directly above my head.

"Can you hear that?" I asked.

"What?"

"The helicopter. This always happens when my cousin John is behind something that is happening on the earth plane. He communicates through the number 22, Ben and Jerry ice cream, helicopters and writing in the dust."

"Hilary, you'll have to explain that," laughed Kate.

"Yes it must sound a bit crazy. From my own personal experiences surrounding the death of loved ones, it seems to me that the deceased person shows how they will indicate their ongoing presence and their guidance shortly after passing over. In the days between my father's death and his funeral, the clocks started playing up, and tiny black flies kept appearing around the various members of the family. Now whenever a clock stops in front of my eyes or when a small black fly buzzes around my head, I know it's my dad making me aware of his presence. When my cousin John died at the age of 60 I was very upset and shed bucket loads of tears. At his funeral, as I stood at the side of his grave I noticed a helicopter hovering in the sky nearby. It had always been John's dream to learn how to fly a helicopter but he had died without realising this dream. Then, as I pulled out of the church car park at the end of the service (still in tears) my exit was suddenly blocked by a huge bin lorry. I had no choice but to turn my engine off and sit and wait for the men to empty the bins. As the bins were placed and the tailgate rose, I saw that someone had written a message in the dust in large capital letters. SMILE. From that day on, whenever I see a message written in dust I know that the chances are that it is a message from John. On the car journey back to my home I was stuck behind a Ben and Jerry's ice cream van. My daughter – who was in the car with me – used to go to the shops with John and he always bought her Ben and Jerry's ice cream. He was the only person who did so."

"I guess you need to be really aware to notice those things happening, to be really in the moment," said Kate.

"Yes, you're right," I replied.

I have only once been back to visit John's grave as I realise that although the remains of his physical body are there, he is not there. As I tidied his grave and placed fresh flowers on it, I couldn't help but notice a helicopter in the sky above. Once again, the link between John and a helicopter. However, the clearest sign from John appeared while I was sitting at my kitchen table. John's death had been a shock because he was neither ill nor old when he died. I was musing over the difficulties of dealing with sudden and unexpected death when I clearly heard his voice. "Count the days," he said. I knew he meant me to count how many days he had lived so I did so. Using the website 'www.daysbetween-dates.com' I calculated how many days he had been on planet earth and was astounded to discover that the answer was 22,222. From that time onwards I knew that the repeated number 2 would be a guidance sign from John but, because of the fact that my dad was already using the stopping and starting of clocks to communicate with me, the time of 22:22 now holds great significance for me. I believe that John and my father are working together to guide me from the astral plane.

"Anyway, we're getting side tracked. You said you were going to ring me."

"Oh yes. I wanted to tell you about this talk I went to last night. It was about the First World War. Of course I'm sure you know all about why the war started don't you?"

I had to confess that I didn't have a clue. I'd never really thought about it. All I knew was that the war had a link with 11/11 because the ending of the First World War was 11/11/1918. The peace treaty was signed at 11am. So that's the 11th hour of the 11th day of the 11th month. I also knew that Harry Patch, Britain's last war veteran had recently died. At the age of 100 he had broken his decades-long silence on the First World War to describe it as 'legalised mass murder'. He died 11 years after breaking his silence at the age of 111.

"The whole first world war thing started to kick off when this guy called Franz Ferdinand went to visit Sarajevo where he was murdered," explained Kate.

"Who's he?" I asked.

"He was the heir to the Austrian Empire. Austria thought that Serbia was responsible for his murder so the Austrians asked Germany for help in defeating Serbia along with its ally Russia. Then Germany attacked France and it all started to get out of hand with Germany, Austria, Belgium, France, Russia, and England all getting involved. But that's not what I wanted to tell you. I wanted to tell you the incredible story of Franz's car number plate."

"Car number plate..." I repeated in astonishment as I was enveloped in a tingling sensation.

"Yes, the car in which he was driven to his death. It wasn't an official car. It was some car that had been loaned to him for his day in Sarajevo by an officer of the Austrian army transport corps. Well, this guy that was giving the talk put up a picture of the car on the screen and I gasped. I saw it straight away."

"Saw what?"

"The number plate. The lecturer told us to look at the number plate of the car. It was A111118. He told us that the war ended on 11/11/18 so that the number plate was almost like a prediction. Get it? 11/11/18. And he said that the letter A stood for Armistice."

"Is this a true story?" I asked, hardly able to believe what I was hearing.

"Yes, sure, it's absolutely true. You can go and see the car. It's still in a museum somewhere. In fact it had been sitting in the museum for years and nobody had noticed this massive coincidence until a British visitor pointed it out to the museum attendant relatively recently."

I knew that this incredible story was being told to me so that I would take particular note of the number plate on the car outside the house. That was the ultimate sign. My sign had been given and I was being asked to take the leap of faith. 'A' is the first letter of the alphabet and I had already made the connection between the initials AA and the number 11. To me that number plate could be interpreted as 11 11 111. I know I had asked for signs around the number 33 but the 11:11 is the sign of 'Divine Alignment'. I couldn't begin to imagine how the universe had managed to place a car with such a number plate right outside the rental property. This was pretty high in the top 10 miracles of the year for me.

"Now I know why I had to ring you," I said. "I'm really clear on the way forward now. I'm going to take the house. Thank you so much, Kate."

I pressed the 'end call' button and saw that the time was 13:13. It had taken a few days to quash the interference from my human self, but in that moment, I surrendered to the sign and accepted the contract on the house. Deep down I knew I would. I don't know why my mind still thinks it has a say in matters like this! As soon as I had committed to renting the cottage, it was like a torrent of energy being released. I was flooded with the feeling that I had done the right thing. People say that they feel things in their bones but I felt this in every atom of my being. After all the mental torment over the decision I had finally managed to take the required leap of faith. It would be some weeks later before I realised that I done so on the 330th day of the year.

Chapter 32

The Cove

It was 28th November and it was a leap year. Kate emailed me to remind me that it was the 333rd day of the year. "Yes," I replied. "And there are 33 days until the end of 2012."

There were only 2 weeks to go before 12/12/12. This was the last of the triple dates that had started on 01/01/01. The gates were being opened on each of the triple dates from 01/01/01 through to 12/12/12. I see these gates as doorways of consciousness. Each one that opens allows Humanity to raise their consciousness to a higher level until it reached Divine consciousness and Oneness with all that is.

I had made a decision. I committed to holding 2 ceremonies, one at the Cove and the second at Stanton Drew stone circle. As usual all Hilary's doubts and insecurities made an appearance. However, Hilary was now under the direction of her Divine Self. On that day with its strong '333' link, a knowing washed over me. I had complete clarity accompanied by an instant download of information. The Cove had become disconnected energetically from the main stone circles. I needed to open and prepare the blocked Divine Feminine channel on 12/12 /12 then connect it to main circle as preparation for the main event, which would take place 9 days later on 21/12/12. On that day the main portal opening would take place.

I thought I would ask Laura Button if she would like to be involved in the gatherings as we had worked together at the Uffington White Horse. I also prefer to work with others when running groups rather than working alone.

Hi Laura, I have had some very strong guidance concerning 21st Dec 2012. I have to open a portal at Stanton Drew on that day. Also I would like to do some energy work on the Cove on 12/12/12. It would be great if you wanted to be part of this and could come along with your crystal skulls. If you're up for it I'd really like to get together with you to discuss the ceremony. I'm currently in Clevedon, Somerset, England. Hilary

What I didn't realise when I sent this email was that Laura had been involved in an 11/11/11 ceremony at Stanton Drew. Along with thousands of others around the world she had opened the 11th gateway of ascension. She had already worked with the energies of that site so she was the perfect person to be working with. We posted the following announcements online:

12/12/12 The Cove, Stanton Drew
As a preparation for the 21/12/2012 portal opening at the large stone circle in Stanton Drew, there will be a small gathering at The Cove in the village of Stanton Drew, Somerset, England on 12/12/2012. This is to link the Gateway to the main circle. If you feel prompted to come along to this ceremony please do so. The Cove is adjacent to the Druid Arms pub. This opening will commence at 11am and will last for 11 minutes.

21/12/12 Stanton Drew Stone Circle
Come and join in a celebration to honour the earth on the pivotal day of 21.12.2012. This is the date of the ending of the Mayan calendar. It is the winter solstice, the day that the sun moves into Capricorn. This year that happens at exactly 11:11am GMT.

Bring your chimes, Tibetan bowls, drums, pipes and your voice as we use sound to align and fully open the portal at the second largest stone circle in England. Everybody is welcome... Bring along your crystals if you would like to charge them with ascension energy.

We will be gathering in time for an 11am start. The moment of alignment will be at 11:11am.

Just turn up and join in. It's going ahead whatever the weather.

Further details can be found on my website: www.hilary carter.com

Laura gave me her website details to add to the posters: sapphirebluedragon.co.uk

Sapphire. Of all the precious stones to be, it was the same crystal energy as my own powerful raw sapphire that I had been working with for the previous 3 years. In my experience, crystals are capable of holding massive amounts of energy, and I usually work with a single crystal for years at a time, carrying it with me to sacred sites and holy places. My crystal is then used as a key to unlock certain frequencies, provide protection and raise the vibration at whatever location it is placed in. I saw on her website that Laura had recently qualified as a Quantum Healing Hypnosis practitioner and she was offering sessions at a reduced price.

Cost: As a recently qualified practitioner, I am choosing to offer sessions at a reduced price. The first 10 clients are free of charge. From the 11th client onwards I will continue with the following charging system:

1 @ £11
2 @ **£22**
3 @ £33
4 @ £44
5 @ £55
6 @ £66
7 @ £77
8 @ £88

Session 2 @ £22 was highlighted as it was the next one available. The number 22 was a sign that I needed a session. By the time I got round to asking Laura about it she told me that the £22 session had been taken so the next available one would be £33. That was an even stronger sign as it was Becket's number. I booked my session for December 18th.

The Cove ceremony was a small but particularly beautiful ceremony and it was touchingly feminine. There was a softness in the air despite the weather being overcast and extremely cold. We were in the middle of one of the coldest English winters on record. I borrowed the conch shell from the convent shrine and I also took the nun's bell. 9 of us gathered to decorate the Cove with flowers, shells, candles and offerings. We carefully placed some selected crystals to hold the energy whilst the preparations for the connection took place. We walked in a silent procession from the Cove to the main stone circle, holding the intention that we were linking the gateway stones with the main stone circle. Laura led the procession down the road, past the Druid Arms pub, past the village school and the war monument, along the cul de sac of modern houses, around the outer edges of the stone circle and then we spiralled in towards the very centre. I brought up the rear, protecting the chain of light and ringing the little golden bell as we walked to the main stone circle. Even though I doubt that it was old enough to have belonged to the French nuns, I felt their presence each time I rung that goddess bell. Laura brought her crystal skulls and laid out her medicine wheel in the very centre of the stones. We chanted, said some prayers and then the clouds cleared and the sun shone. The work was done.

By the time I arrived home less than an hour later, my left eye was killing me. It felt as though there was a bit of glass stuck under my eyelid. When I looked in the mirror I saw that my eye was bloodshot and slightly swollen. Bathing it in saline and soothing it with eye drops did nothing to relieve the irritation. I had a restless night, hoping that I would wake in the morning to find a piece of glass sitting neatly in the corner of my eye so that

I could easily remove it. No such luck. It was just as painful in the morning. By the evening I had had enough of the constant irritation and I walked to the outpatients department of the nearby hospital to ask for help. The nurse dropped anaesthetic drops into my eye and brushed a cotton wool bud under the eyelid 4 times, not an experience I would ever want to repeat.

"There's nothing there," she said peering closely at the tip of the cotton bud. "I can't see anything. How does it feel now?"

"Much better," I replied. "I think whatever was there has gone."

In fact nothing had changed. I couldn't feel anything, but that was because the anaesthetic had kicked in. As soon as it began to wear off it was clear that whatever had been there was still there. The following day a lump appeared on the white of my left eye. I just knew that this was to do with the re-opening of the feminine energy at Stanton Drew. It was far too coincidental to be anything else. I had never experienced anything like a lump on my eye in my entire life. On 12/12/12 I had allowed my body to be used as a conduit through which the Divine Feminine energy could connect with the earth within the circle. Stanton Drew, although little known in the 21st-century had been an incredibly important site in its heyday and I knew that certain souls (including Laura and me) had agreed to regenerate the energetic perfection of Stanton in this lifetime.

Around the eye there are entrance and exit point for many of the channels of energy within our human energy system. The stagnation of the Stanton Drew site had manifested in my eye. My own physical eye was being used as the microcosm of the macrocosm and I knew it linked to the heart energy of the earth. Don't ask me how I knew. I just knew. It was the link to zero point within the Fibonacci series of numbers.

It is only recently that the intelligence system of the heart has been discovered. The heart is not just a pumping machine. It is an intel-

ligence system. It is in fact the most intelligent system of all our brains, with its own receptors, its own electromagnetic force, from 45 to 70 times more powerful than the brains of the neocortex, and the only force capable of changing our own DNA.
http://www.wingmakers.co.nz/Fire_Meridian.html

I instinctively knew that the 11:11 was an outer sign of the inner change of the DNA, reprogramming humans with the new consciousness program and this lump on my eye indicated a major DNA shift, not only for me but for Stanton Drew and its counterpart, Stonehenge.

Halfway between the dates 12/12/12 and 21/12/12, I visited the estate agents in Taunton to pick up the key for the cottage in Watchet. That is a symbolic act in itself. I was still looking for keys, keys to the mystery of Becket. There seemed to be keys everywhere.

As I had to walk past the museum of Somerset on my way to collect the key I called in to see the reliquary that contained Becket's blood. I recalled reading that the famous Michael/Mary leyline went straight through Taunton. According to Jim Olcott if you were given a ruler and a map and asked to draw the longest line in Britain without crossing water you will end up with a track that stretches from the tip of Lands End to the Norfolk coast near the town of Hopton. This old straight track is known as the St Michael and St Mary line. The distance from coast to coast between these two end-points of Land's End and Hopton is 365.24 miles precisely. A solar year is 365.242199 days. Coincidence? I don't think so.

Becket, Becket, Becket. Once again his name kept entering my awareness, running through my mind in the same way that the blood runs through my veins. His name wouldn't go away. It was like a mantra, always there in the background. Becket, Becket, Becket. What part did Becket have to play in this unfolding mystery? I needed to find the answer to that question and I needed it answered before 21/12/2012. I was slightly wary about asking Kate about our possible involvement in the life and death of Becket because she's so powerfully intuitive that part of me didn't want to know what part I might have played in that scenario. I was uncomfortably aware of the fact that there were 2 of us and 2 of the knights had been born in Watchet. I obviously considered the fact that Kate and I were the 2 knights but it didn't resonate with my truth. However, the issue needed to be cleared and I refused to come from fear so I asked her. I kept it simple and straight to the point.

Hi Kate, So…I need to run this past you and I need a response before 11:11am on 21/12/2012 (Friday). I'll explain all at a later date. It's a simple question… Do you feel that either of us had any part to play in the murder of Thomas Becket?

Note the time of her response…

Subject: Becket
From: Kate
Date: Mon, 17 Dec 2012 13:31:30 +0000
To: Hilary
I am not getting the feeling that I was one of the knights… BUT when you asked me the question I was very aware of the monk I always 'see' looking down on the dreadful scene and felt that I could be HIM. Am not receiving vibes that you were one of his killers. Are you feeling you might have been?

That was not the first time that Kate had mentioned that feeling of having witnessed the murder. Several times she had spoken of seeing the whole murder scene unfolding before her inner vision. I was certain that she must have been there during the attack and I had a feeling that maybe I had been involved too. I was relieved that she had not implied I was one of the 4 knights but I wanted to know exactly what part I did play, if any. I didn't realise that the answers I was seeking were about to be revealed.

Chapter 33

Quantum Healing Hypnosis

I had booked my hypnosis session for Tuesday 18th December when the moon was in mystical Pisces. Both the moon and Neptune were sitting on my natal sun so I knew I was in for a revelation. Not only that but from the convent in Marine Hill, Clevedon to Laura's place in the High Street, Hanham, Bristol was exactly 33 km so I also knew that Becket would be playing a part in my hypnotic experience.

It was exactly 100 days since Laura and I had first met at the White Horse in Uffington. I lay on the colourful bed in her bohemian house, not far from another holy well, Saint Anne's Well. I had no idea what to expect from my session but as usual I just go with the flow. Laura's voice was gentle and soothing and before long she had enabled me to reach a deep state of being.

"Where are you?" she asked. With closed eyes I looked around my inner world. I was in a street outside a tall house. She had guided me back to a life as a woodcutter. I had died during the Black Death epidemic and I had buried every single member of my family before succumbing to the illness myself and dying in a ditch on the side of the road. During the hypnosis I recalled the names of my 2 little daughters, Genevieve and Jacqueline. I had buried them along with their mother. I had died full of anger towards God for having allowed this to happen. My last words as I left my physical body in that life were, "God has cursed us."

Having experienced that death, Laura asked me to leave it behind.

"Now we want to leave that life and communicate with the consciousness and personality of Hilary. I want to speak to Hilary's Higher Self. May I?" she asked.

"Yes."

"The Higher Self takes care of Hilary and has the record of everything that Hilary has ever experienced in all lifetimes she has ever lived. Do I have permission to ask questions?"

"Yes."

"What was going on with Hilary's eye after Stanton Drew?"

"The microcosm and the macrocosm. There is an underground channel from Glastonbury to Stanton Drew. Also Stonehenge."

"What is the function of Stanton Drew?"

"It's a major energy centre. Heart Goddess. It's a vital centre."

"Are there special codes that we link into when we do the work at Stanton Drew? Is there anything you want to say about that?"

"You are the code."

"We are the code?"

"You are coded. Programmed. Your physical bodies need to be there. You are the keys that unlock the energy."

"So it's important that we are physically on these sites?"

"You have no idea. Repeat. You have no idea of the importance. It is essential for you to be there."

"What if we were on a different site?"

"There is no what if, only what is."

"I want to ask an important question. Hilary wants to know what Thomas Becket is trying to tell her. Has he got a message for her?"

"Forgive yourself."

"And is this connected to the knights who killed Thomas Becket?"

"Yes."

"Was Hilary involved in the murder?"

"Yes."

"Who was she? Was she one of the knights who killed him?"

There was a long pause at this point. Later I understood the reason for the pause because Thomas Becket stepped in at this point.

"Not one of the knights. She is involved. She is carrying guilt. She feels she played a part in my death. She thinks she could have said something to prevent it. But it was my choice. She is carrying guilt. She needs to forgive herself."

The wording of the answer, the inclusion of 'my' in the answer was what suggested that this was a direct channel to Becket. Guilt. This journey had all started so many months earlier when Kate had sent me the photo of the red tipped swords that hung in Canterbury cathedral and she had titled it GUILT.

Becket had come through to tell me not to feel guilt. Firstly I didn't kill him and secondly I couldn't have prevented it because it was his choice to die in the way he did at the cathedral. I had carried that guilt through many lifetimes in the same way that the families of his killers had carried that shame down through the generations. Now I understood that it was Becket's choice to die in the way that he did. He had chosen to spill his blood on the floor of Canterbury Cathedral for the greater good of all. It was his sacrifice.

"It was his choice," said Laura meaningfully as if to hammer the message home. "He forgives you and you need to forgive yourself. Are you ready to release that guilt now?"

"Yes I am."

"So we ask Thomas Becket to help Hilary to let go of that..."

"It had to be that way for his miracles to be manifest," I explained to Laura. "It was for the highest good of all."

"Exactly," replied Laura. "I understand."

"Me too," I replied with a huge sense of relief.

So, it appears that although I was involved in Becket's murder in some way, I didn't kill him. I was carrying guilt because of a feeling that I could have prevented it happening. I couldn't understand why I felt that way. I needed more clarity on the issue. I wanted to know the full story, but I would just have to wait for more to be revealed in due course.

Chapter 34

The Ascension

3 days after my Quantum Healing Hypnosis the pivotal date of 21st December finally arrived. This was the big day, the long awaited ending of the Mayan calendar. The cold woke me up early and when I looked out of the window of the convent of Mercy I saw that everything was covered with a deep layer of frost. Then my phone rang. It was Laura. She had flu and wouldn't be able to join in the celebration so, like it or not I would have to lead the ceremony alone.

I scraped down the car with frozen fingers and turned on the ignition. The clock was on 10:00 and the temperature inside the car was 10 degrees so the illuminated display read: 10 00 10. The trip was on 111.3 and the milometer on 30996. The time was 9.55am. I registered all those numbers as I always do. To tread the path of number as I do requires acute observation of everything that is appearing in my everyday world. Full awareness in every moment enables the number signs to be seen and noted.

The sun was weak and watery. I drove through the countryside, a silver land, the trees lightly brushed with winter frosts, half hidden in a haze of freezing fog. It looked beautiful but it was painfully cold. The flood warning signs had been replaced with highway warning signs depicting snowflakes because now the floods had iced over. All the roads were like huge skating rinks.

I suddenly started singing the mantra Om Tara in the car on the way to Stanton Drew. I used to play it regularly when I first started teaching yoga but I hadn't sung or chanted it for several years. Because of my yoga studies I knew that in Indian Hinduism, the star goddess Tara is a manifestation of the queen of time, Kali. What I didn't know as I sang my way to the circle was that Tara was also the name of the Mother Goddess in the Druidic religion. Stanton is a Tara site. I cannot prove it but I know it.

I pulled up outside the gate of Stanton Drew stone circle and collected my stuff together. As I reached to pick up my bowl from the back seat of the car I saw something glinting in the light. It was a gold ring in the form of a plaited rope. It had obviously fallen from my mother's skeletal finger as her physical body had become so thin that all of her rings had dropped off, including her wedding ring. I picked it up and examined it. It had belonged to my auntie, Nan, mother of my cousin John who had lived on planet earth for exactly 22,222 days. I slipped it on my little finger and it was a perfect fit. I knew that the heart meridian flowed down that particular finger so I decided to wear it for the day as it would link me with my ancestral line.

Using my sapphire crystal as pendulum I dowsed for the centre of the circle to find the right place for the central altar. The moment I found it my phone rang. It was Mike Handcock, the friend who had been involved in the clearing at Dracula's Castle. He was calling me from Uluru in the centre of Australia to tell me that his group was connecting with my group and that he loved me. I told him I loved him too as I had for so many lives. Not a personal, possessive, sexual or co-dependant love but a pure soul love that transcends all that. Love. That is what ascension is all about and so of course it had to manifest within the ceremony. Having circled the site with sound and incense I then created a central altar and the group began to gather. There were over 30 people there, from babes in arms through to elderly couples and all ages in between. As we stood there chanting Om I became aware of literally thousands of other beings joining us in this glorious chorus, including my own ancestors. I chanted Om Tara as I spiralled the energy inwards and released the block within the Divine Feminine.

We began to move as one in an anti-clockwise circle. A

Goddess in a wheelchair held the central space by repeating the Gayetri mantra. It was, as had been directed, a joyous ceremony. We sang Lennon's 'All You Need is Love' as love is the critical ingredient in the manifestation of the new earth and the core of our true nature. We are beings of Love.

"All you need is love, all you need is love,
All you need is love, love, love is all you need."

Then Bob Marley's...

"Emancipate yourself from mental slavery,
None but our self can free our minds."

I then took the bowl of crystals from the central altar and offered one to everyone. Even the little children plunged their hands into the bowl and plucked a treasure, for treasures they certainly were. These were ascension crystals, imbued with cosmic energy that could be used for healing or as pendulums as each one had a hole drilled through the centre. Never again will such crystals be manifested for the day of ascension will not be repeated. We ended the ceremony dancing and singing, filling the area with joy and love as we shared the blessed food from the central altar of the circle. Still filled with the beautiful energy of the ceremony, my friend Sarah and I called in at the local church. This time the bible was open at the beginning of 'The Song of Songs of Solomon'. This beautiful part of the Old Testament is thought to be an allegory of God's love for humankind or of the intensity of Divine love within the human heart. It's a book all about love and as such I felt it was a perfect ending to the Stanton Drew ceremony.

Whilst I was releasing the blocked energy in England, on the other side of the earth my soul brother Mike was toning sacred sounds in the cave of the earth mother. He was with his group within a very sophisticated portal at Uluru, aligned to the rising and setting sun. As Mike stood on the stone altar he realised that directly above him was a bright star. Using the star map app on his iPhone he pointed it directly upwards to try and identify the star. At that precise moment his phone screen went black and froze for 24 hrs. His camera immediately shut down, never to work again, despite the fact that his phone was only 3 weeks old.

Chapter 35

Becket's Birthday

Later that day, after a leisurely lunch I drove out to Woodspring to join Victoria and Andrew at their beautiful property. As I drove through their gate I remembered the excitement of my last visit. I had been in my old car and the milometer had reached 111,111 as I drove down their lane. Now I was in my new car and I would have to drive more than 80,000 miles before I would see that line up of 1s again.

As I drove into the driveway I could see Victoria busy emptying the water from the fire pit. She had just completed a bush craft course and her newly acquired skills were already coming in handy. With great expertise she managed to set a fire despite the dampness of the earth and soon it was blazing. She hung a pot of vegetarian stew from a tripod above the flames, waiting for it to heat through.

I asked Andrew and Victoria to tell me a bit more about their house and the land on which it sat because I couldn't understand why their place looked quite modern, certainly much more recent than the old stone building adjacent to the house.

"What's that old building? I asked.

"That's Woodspring Priory. It's now owned by the Landmark Trust and they rent it out as a holiday let," replied Andrew. "It's reputed to be haunted by 2 ghosts. One, a lady, walks in the garden on the full moon, and the other clanks the chains in the church."

"So you don't live in the priory."

"Our house and field sit in the grounds of the original priory. The dip in the field that our goats occupy is the monk's old trout pond. Our house is on the fringes of the old priory grounds. It is rumoured that it has been built on the very site of the original wooden temporary building that the monks used while the main structure was being built. The knight that was one of Thomas Becket's murderers is believed to be buried in one of three places, either in our field, St Thomas's Head or somewhere else entirely. Geo Phys checks have found nothing yet."

"That's interesting. I was under the impression that the knights had been buried in Solomon's Temple."

"I guess nobody knows for sure where they ended up. The priory had an open day last month and it was interesting to meet the head archaeologist of Somerset, who showed us a Norman headstone that was found in the field next to us. It suggests that even the priory was built on established sacred ground. When this area was cut off by the tide, it was clearly ideal for those wishing to escape the confines of society."

"So what's that mound of earth near the fire pit?" I asked.

"The mound in our garden is part of the priory grounds, but no one has suggested what it could be. There is a lot of rubble about, so it could be a boundary wall but nobody knows for sure."

I had to accept that all my questions couldn't necessarily be answered. Anyway, it was only my mind that wanted to know. At least my heart was content, knowing that I was spending the evening of December 21st 2012 in such a special place.

We sat in a circle around the fire pit. There were only 6 of us, 5 women and Andrew. It was so beautiful to be outdoors on an English December evening and we were fortunate to be able to be out. This was the first time for weeks that it hadn't been raining or snowing. 2012 had been a record-breaking year for rainfall in Somerset. The moon glowed softly through the mist and we could hear the sound of chiming bells in the distance. There was a stillness in the air, a kind of pause, as though the cosmos was waiting for something to happen. The rain held off until 22:00 hours, allowing us time to mark this significant day with an outdoor ceremony. We started by clearing the space with incense and then we chanted together as a group. I was mindful of the fact that I was sitting on sacred ground with a direct link to Thomas Becket. How blessed I felt.

Each of us took some paper and a pen and wrote 3 things we wished to leave behind from that moment in time. Having openly shared our truth, we then burned our papers in the fire. We then wrote 3 things we were grateful for and 3 things we were open to bringing into our lives. 3 lots of 3. 3,3,3. Becket... As we sat there around the blazing fire within the shadow of the tower of the adjacent priory I suddenly remembered that December 21st was a significant date for another reason. It was Becket's birthday.

When the rain started we moved indoors and sat by the lounge fire in silent meditation. It was then that I became aware of the chain of guilt that hung heavy in the energy field of the site. After all, this place had been built through the emotion of guilt by the Fitzurse family 2 generations after the death of Reginald Fitzurse. The guilt had been handed down through the generations from father to son, the descendants of Fitzurse tainted in some way by their blood link with one of Becket's murderers. Even the family of Kate's friend felt that they were in some way tarnished by the actions of their ancestors despite the fact that the murder had happened over 1000 years earlier. How strong that chain of guilt can be.

I entered a deep state of meditation very quickly. I could feel the kundalini energy in my spine buzzing and I began swaying from side to side. It was a rapid swaying and probably impercep-tible to the naked eye. The charge going through me was intense and I immediately entered the realm of no-time. My physical body was being used as the switch that enabled the breaking of the chain to take place. This was work that I had elected to do before incarnating into the English female body of Hilary Carter. The chain of guilt connected to this sacred ground was released very quickly in earth time measurement and in doing so many souls were set free. They were souls that were attached to this particular place (many of them monks) through guilt. I felt them enter the circle of light that the 6 of us had created by sitting in a circle around the fire. In a way it was not unlike the Havan fire at the Ashram. The fire was necessary to burn away the dross and facilitate the transformation. I never cease to be amazed at the perfection of the universe. 6 souls, all of whom were carrying the amount of light within their cells that was necessary to do this work had been brought to this fire within the house located on the ground of the priory on the birthday of Thomas Becket which just happened to be the day of the Galactic earth shift. Incredible! Not only that, but I remembered what Kate had said at the beginning of this number journey.

"Then I got the impression that this is something to do with freeing those who are caught in guilt – well everyone is really – to free those in this life but also those in the so called next, those no longer in the physical".

So once more I had been used as a switch to connect the Universal Light to the earth and again I recalled the words of Kate's son when he had said, "Where is the switch?" at 11:11 am at the beginning of the year. The function of a switch is to break and connect the flow of electricity. The function of a key is to unlock something. Maybe I was both a key and a switch.

2012 was drawing to a close and what a year it had been. I had spent a month travelling in Italy, visiting Lamezia, Rome, Naples and Sicily. This was followed by a trip to Turin. Then I was in France for almost 2 months, followed by a trip to Ibiza for the 11/11/12. In between my trips abroad I had travelled to various places in England including Salisbury, Devon, London, Kewstoke, Taunton, Bristol, Canterbury, Bournemouth, Brighton, Avebury, Uffington and Stanton Drew. After all that travelling I was about to land in the small and somewhat obscure little town of Watchet. I wondered why the numbers had sent me there.

Chapter 36

Olympus and Pegasus

I fought my way down through the overgrown convent garden. It was slippery with the moss that had flourished due to the damp weather. I carefully replaced the large conch shell on the marble slab in front of Mother Mary, giving thanks for the loan of it. I sat down on the stone bench where I had received the car number-plate sign from Kate regarding the move to Watchet. In front of me where once there had been trees, shrubs and roses was a large, newly laid concrete car park. Already the car parking spaces had been marked out for the luxury apartments. I could see the words 'St Teresa' carved into the stone path from where I sat but I guessed that the path, along with the crazy paving and the walls of natural stone, would probably soon be under concrete too. The walled garden was being dug up with a huge orange digger. No longer would anyone be able to look out over the walled convent garden because the foundations for the new houses would soon be laid.

I went to the library to look at the planning documents to see if there was any mention of the shrine being protected. There wasn't. However I learned that the application was number 11/P/1777 and the decision date of the application was...11/11/11. Do you see that immense synchronicity? This is fact, not fiction and anyone can prove facts like this as the documents exist in the physical world. The number signs appear in my life so dramatically and so consistently that I sometimes have to pinch myself. I am living such an incredible life. Maybe you are too, but unless you keep your awareness in the moment then you will miss the number signs that might be surrounding you.

It was time to leave the convent. I had been guided there by intuition and the car milometer. I had put aside all limiting thoughts and acted on the signs. Through that leap of faith I had...

Finally discovered the miracle of the Spanish convent.

Brought the goddess energy into my life.

Been gifted a golden Goddess bell for ceremonial use.

Experienced communal living.

Been given even more information regarding the Black Madonna by Patrick as I had discovered that Patrick was still alive and well. The funeral I had attended was obviously a different Patrick from Liverpool.

It was time to move on, to flow. I removed the 3 convent keys from my key ring and returned them to the estate agents called Templer. Handing over those 3 keys felt very symbolic. There is something deep about keys, especially in triplicate... I now held in my hand a shiny, brand new key. The locks to the Watchet house had recently been changed because the previous occupant had been a problem tenant who had not paid any rent and had run up huge gas and electricity bills. There was only one door to the house and that was at the front. I unlocked it, and once again the first thing I noticed was the smell. It was a putrid stink of damp. The carpets were even more worn and grimy than I had remembered and I noticed that there were cigarette burns in quite a few places. The damp in the kitchen was so severe that it extended to head height. The decrepit old cooker was caked in grease and all the light switches and electric sockets were stiff with dirt. I could see daylight through the ill-fitting front door. I stood in the lounge on the top floor with the wind whipping through the rotten window and the flies buzzing around my ears. As soon as I put the heating on the windows began to run with condensation. I was overwhelmed with remorse.

"What have I done?" I whispered. "I can't possibly live in a place like this."

I had to remind myself that it was no-thought that had led me to the house and I had to stay in the realm of no-thought to be able to deal with it. In other words, I needed to trust the process and focus on the positive. Energy follows thought. Whatever we focus on grows in power through mental energy. So if we focus on anything that we deem to be imperfect, we actually tie ourselves to that very imperfection. Instead we can focus on perfection. I tried to do that with the house. I focussed on the view and the location rather than the cigarette burns and the damp. The saving grace of the property was definitely the view from the top floor window. From that window I had an unobstructed panoramic view of the 1000 year old harbour and the sea beyond. I was only a few metres from the harbour's edge. If it wasn't for the lifeboat station directly in front of the property I would have been on the harbour itself. Thankfully the lifeboat station was not a high building which is why I could see the harbour over its rooftop and it served to shelter my bedroom from the worst of the storms. It was January and there weren't many boats moored. Directly in my line of vision were 2 larger vessels. I narrowed by eyes to try to make out their names but they were too far away.

Later that day I went for a wander. On my way back home I walked to the end of the harbour wall to where the 2 large boats were moored. Through the mist I saw 'OLYMPUS' written on the side of the large white boat. Adjacent to Olympus was large black vessel. I could just make out the writing. 'PEGASUS'. Pegasus again. The harbour masters boat was called Nemesis and that was next to one called Achilles. I shook my head in disbelief. There was no doubt about it – my Higher Self was leading me towards mythology.

Chapter 37

Holy Cross Chapel

The Watchet house, like the French convent, was unique. It was only after I moved in that I realised it was another tower, tall and narrow, having 3 floors with only one room on each floor exactly the same as the convent. Unlike the French convent which sat on a large plot of land, the house had no outside space (not even a balcony) so I soon adopted the well as my garden. The holy well drew me like a moth to a flame. I couldn't keep away. The draw was definitely magnetic in nature. Most days I climbed the hill to spend time by the water because it was as if my soul clicked into place whenever I was there. It had been a sacred site long before the Christian monk Decuman had arrived in Watchet from Wales during the 7th-century.

I explored the town whenever I could. I walked every inch of the area as I got to know my new surroundings. There was a large paper mill on the edge of town, between the harbour and the well. Steam and noxious smells emanated from this industrial site. Paper making in Watchet dates back to 1652, but machines weren't introduced until 1869. Sometimes I was very aware of the sound of the mill whilst I was at the well and at other times I didn't notice it at all. It seems as if Kate was right when she said that we choose what we tune in to.

I was actually looking for the local municipal dump a couple of miles from Watchet when I happened upon a signpost for Sampford Brett. Richard Le Breton (one of Becket's killers) was also known as Richard Brett so I called in at the church as I thought there could be a connection. Hanging on the wall of the church (St George's) was a comprehensive family tree of the Brett family tracing the Brett family from 1095 to 1853. It clearly stated who Richard le Breton was.

Sir Richard Le Brett Kt. Lord of Hescombe & Williton (murderer).
Richard Le Brett, with Reginald FitzUrse from Williton and two
other knights murdered Thomas a Becket in Canterbury Cathedral
on 29 December 1170. Woodspring Priory (Near Kewstoke) was
founded in 1210 by his family in expiation and dedicated to St
Thomas.

And of course that's where Andrew was living, on the land of the original Kewstoke priory. Andrew is my number 33 man and this is where the whole 33 journey had started. Although it was Reginald who led the murderers, it was Richard le Breton who hit Becket with such force that he broke his sword. The family tree in the church uses the spelling of Richard le Brett but he is known variously as Le Brett, Le Brito or Le Breton.

Arriving home later that day I sat down with a cup of tea and my eyes were immediately drawn to a book on the bookshelf called *The Key to Solomon's Key*. I glanced at my phone: 3.33pm. I turned to page 111:

Solomon's secret 3:
Human beings evolve and with intent can accelerate the evolutionary process. This secret has been the foundation for the spiritual practices of the East for millennia but in the West it has been successfully supressed by religious doctrine and cultural interests since the 5th-century CE.

That is exactly what the established Christian church had done. It had doled out a watered down version of the truth, thereby hoodwinking (to use Kate's word) generations of people. The book that drew my eyes that day had literally fallen into my hands in the bookshop some months earlier. I always buy books that fall on my head or at my feet as I believe that books carry energy and can actually make contact with us in this way. Many years ago I was reading an old theosophical book from the 19th-

century and the author (obviously long dead) began to read the words to me in a gravelly Scottish voice. Another time I was reading a book by the yogi Theos Bernard and a blue light appeared around the book itself.

This was the third appearance of Solomon so I allowed the information to sink in deeply. I knew that 'with intent we can accelerate the evolutionary process' because that was my intention, to evolve from being a human being within the third dimension to becoming a cosmic being with access to all dimensions.

The next day, as I lay on the bedroom floor listening to the clinking of the yachts in the harbour I became aware of the sound of a bell ringing. It was a thin, tinny sound, coming from the present day Holy Cross Chapel. It was a Wednesday morning and communion was being held in the room above the museum. Curiosity took me up the stairs and I attended the service. We all sat in a circle and followed the order of service in the prayer book. The vicar offered the bread and wine to each of us in turn whilst we remained seated, but when she reached me, she dropped the bread on the floor. A startled hush fell on the small congregation. Before anyone could do anything I just picked it up and ate it.

The following week it was a male vicar. He placed the bread in my hand and this time it completely disappeared. We searched everywhere. We looked under the chair and behind the chair. I stood up but it wasn't on the chair. I couldn't find it. Eventually I located it up my sleeve. Dropping the host twice seemed significant and I took it as a sign not to go to the Holy Cross Chapel any more. However, before I came to this decision I asked the vicar about the history of the chapel.

"This building used to be the market place and then the downstairs was used as an ironmongers shop," he explained.

"So they converted part of the ancient Holy Cross Chapel into a shop?" I asked.

"No. This isn't the original Holy Cross Chapel. Nobody knows where that one was located. The original one was a chantry chapel, built by the Fitzurse family after the death of Reginald Fitzurse. You probably know that Reginald Fitzurse was one of the knights who murdered Thomas Becket."

"Yes, I do, but I don't know what a chantry chapel is."

"It's a chapel that employs a priest to sing mass for the benefit of the departed soul of a deceased person. You see, in those days you either went to heaven or hell when you died. Obviously they expected Reginald Fitzurse to be in danger of going to hell because of what he'd done so the family paid for the chapel to be built and for mass to be said for his soul. Normally the priest would have been paid for his services once or twice a week. This particular chapel was unusual because the family paid for a full time priest. Full time, every day, praying for the soul of Fitzurse. They believed that Reginald's soul was in purgatory, a kind of 'holding house' for his soul until enough prayers had been said to allow him into heaven. He was deemed to be in need of an awful lot of prayers because of what he had done. They believed that through prayer his soul could eventually be cleansed, a kind of post-death purification. The family also had to give away a lot of their land to the Knights Templars, including land in Watchet. As well as the Chantry chapel in the centre of Watchet they also built St Decuman's Church, which Richard Le Breton and Reginald Fitzurse then gave to Wells Cathedral. It wasn't just the disgraced knights that had to do penances. Even after their deaths their families had to carry on trying to make amends for the murder."

That would explain why Andrew's Woodspring Priory had been built by the grandson of Fitzurse. The guilt was being handed down through the generations. Now I understood why the local school in Watchet was called the Knights Templar School. It had been built on land originally given to the Order of the Knights Templar by Reginald Fitzurse.

"The Chapel of the Holy Cross had other buildings with it and all were sold in 1548. The other buildings gradually became ruins and their exact whereabouts are not now known," continued the vicar.

The 'Chapell of the Holy Crosse of Wachet' is mentioned several times in old records and there is evidence that a chantry was founded in the chapel. The actual site of the chapel is unknown but it would be reasonable to assume that it was somewhere near the harbour around which practically all the medieval town was situated.
– A History of Watchet by A. L. Wedlake

It could be that my house had been built on the actual site of the chapel. I was located in the historic part of town and near to the harbour. The records show that my house had been built circa 1825 on a garden. Maybe this garden had once been the garden of the old chapel. It certainly would not surprise me if numbers had led me to the place where all those prayers had been said for many hundreds of years for the family of Fitzurse. I had come to dissolve that chain of guilt into the light of love. My presence at this location was releasing the entire Fitzurse family through all generations from their guilt. The guilt had extended out to all those who in some way felt that they were tainted because of their association or connection with the murderers of Thomas Becket. I had the distinct feeling that I was needed at this particular site at exactly 33.3 degrees of longitude for a minimum of 333 days. By then the chain would be released and my work in Watchet would be over.

Chapter 38

Wreaths of Success

Numbericity is the word that I have invented to describe my way of living, the way that combines the appearance of numbers with synchronicity. The trip to Monreale was a perfect example of numbericity. I had wanted to visit Monreale when I had been in Sicily the previous year because I knew that the earliest known artistic representation of Becket anywhere in the world could be found in Monreale Cathedral. Also, the Sicilian Cathedral of Marsala near Palermo is dedicated to Saint Thomas of Canterbury and I would have liked to have seen that. I don't really understand why Kate and I hadn't made Marsala and Monreale our priority on our visit to Sicily the year before. Maybe it was something to do with timing and celestial alignments. But, in the same way that Turin had niggled at my consciousness, Monreale began to do the same thing. I had this really strong intuitive feeling that I needed to go, even though it meant going all the way back to Sicily from my new home in Watchet, Somerset, England. In 2012 I had been in Rome for March 15th (the Ides of March). In 2013 I knew I was to be in Sicily.

I googled 'Monreale' and the first page to come up was TripAdvisor. At the top of the page the number 333 appeared in large, bold letters, '333 reviews of Monreale Cathedral, the number one tourist attraction'. There was the synchronicity. 333. It was such a clear sign that I simply booked my flight. I didn't even think about it for a moment. I wasn't going to put myself through the mental torture I had suffered over the moving to Watchet decision. I booked the flights then it was done. My mind had no say in the matter. The hotel search later that day brought up exactly 33 hotels at Stansted airport, which was my confirmation sign.

I invited Kate along for the journey and as usual when our energies combine, the number signs were rampant. We were drowning in numbers. Of course it helped that we were going to be travelling in the 3rd month of the year 2013 so there were lots of 0s, 1s, 2s and 3s in all the dates.

The day that we committed to our journey by booking our flights there was a news flash. Pope Benedict had suddenly and unexpectedly announced his resignation. A couple of hours after his shock announcement St Peter's Basilica was hit by lightning. I must say that was a confirmation sign that I hadn't seen coming.

Because of the 'Hilaria Joy' link with Cybele and the fact that the statue of St Peter was holding a key, I was on red alert concerning the unfolding events in Rome. I saw the lightning as a positive sign that the light of truth could not be held back.

On 10th March 2013 I set off for London's Stansted airport. My plan was to drive to the nearest railway station in the town of Bridgwater, leave the car at the station and take the train to London. As I stepped out of the Watchet house into the wet and windy day I noticed a sheet of paper lying on my doorstep. It was so wet that it was stuck to my doorstep but it wasn't crumpled up. It was lying there perfectly straight, almost as if somebody had carefully laid it down for me. I picked it up very gently so that it would not tear. It was the frontispiece of a very old Children's encyclopaedia.

I keep six honest serving-men
(They taught me all I knew)
Their names are What and Why and When
And How and Where and Who.
I send them over land and sea,
I send them east and west;
But after they have worked for me,
I give them all a rest.
–Rudyard Kipling

I laughed. I hoped I was being told that I could have a rest from travelling after this Sicilian trip.

I parked my car at the railway station where it would need to stay for over 2 weeks. The milometer was on 32697. I thought that was meaningless until I realised that it would reach 33,000 miles in exactly 33 miles time. That reminded me that I could look at numbers in another way, not just how they appear in front of me but I could add and subtract them too. The trip meter was on 33 and the time was 10:33. The temperature gauge read 3 degrees centigrade. The flight from London to Palermo was on 12/03/2013 so I was surrounded by 1s, 2s and 3s as I left.

As I set off, I had a sense of excitement. "Siclily the key to everything." Why would Goethe have said that? And what were Medusa and the triskelion doing on the Sicilian flag?

There was a sticker of laurel wreath beside my seat on the train so I carefully unpeeled it and stuck it on my notebook. At Stansted airport there was another laurel wreath sticker stuck on the side of the escalator. Then, as I emerged into the check in hall I was confronted with an enormous picture of Pegasus on a poster advertising Pegasus airlines. At this point in time I still hadn't unravelled the mythical messages I was receiving regarding Pegasus, Apollo and Medusa.

I met Kate at the airport.

"Look at my boarding passes," she exclaimed. I looked. One was number 11 and the other was 111. "You've got mine," I joked. It was clear that her own personal 11:11 wake-up call was manifesting. I showed her the laurel wreath sticker that I had unpeeled from the side of the train. As I did so an alarm went off. There had already been an alarm at the railway station. Alarms seemed to be going off all over the place. Not only that, they were linking to the laurel wreath. I had to find the message.

"I wonder what a laurel wreath represents" I said.

"It's very Roman. You always see pictures of Romans wearing them. I think it represents success or crowning glory. I'll look it up."

Within minutes Kate had found the information we needed on her smart phone.

"It says that a wreath is a symbol of the God Apollo."

"Apollo… The Temple of Apollo at Siracusa last time we were in Sicily…"

Kate continued reading from her phone.

"In the Roman world wreaths were used to represent a person's achievements and status. Normally they used laurel for the wreaths. The Greek myth describes how Apollo fell in love with the nymph Daphne and pursued her. She asked Perseus for help so he turned her into a laurel tree. After that day, Apollo always wore a wreath of laurel on his head. Laurel wreaths became associated with what Apollo embodied: victory, achievement and status."

"It's a good sign for this journey then. Any mention of Pegasus or Olympus?" I queried.

"No. But I'll take a look…here…it says that Pegasus flew to mount Olympus."

"Those are the names of the 2 boats moored in Watchet harbour!" I exclaimed. "They're the two biggest boats in the harbour and they're moored right next to each other."

"…and Pegasus was allowed to stay on Olympus and was entrusted with the task of transporting thunderbolts and lightning for Zeus, the king of the Gods," continued Kate.

I was pleased to have found a link between Pegasus and Olympus. We passed many more Pegasus posters on the way to the gate and each time I saw one I felt as if he was laughingly poking me in the ribs.

Chapter 39

The Royal Palace

We were probably flying over Rome at the same time as the first vote for the new Pope was taking place and I could well have been over Rome when I was given the following download during the flight:

12:12pm. You are working on the very heart of the suppression of the divine feminine energy of the planet. Once this is released it will be the last task on Italian soil. You will see 111, 222 and 333 and all combinations of these 3 numbers as they all merge into one because all of existence manifests as number. Zero point is the heart and the heart is zero point. You hear alarms everywhere because the time is now. The time is here. Wake up.

During this, our second visit to Sicily, Kate and I were going to spend 3 nights in Palermo near the Monreale Cathedral followed by 7 nights in an apartment overlooking the sea in the quiet resort of Balestrate. From Balestrate we would take a day trip to visit the Cathedral of Marsala, dedicated to Thomas Becket. We were to fly directly into the Falcone-Borsellino airport in Palermo, named after 2 judges who had been murdered by the Mafia. They blew up the car that Falcone was travelling in, killing him and his wife. I had seen the photos of the car. The number plate was still visible after the explosion: 1166.

"Cabin crew prepare for landing," announced the captain as we approached our destination. I looked out of the airplane window onto the lights of the city below. Palermo, the centre of the Mafia's operations. I wondered how it would be feel to be there. I was about to find out. Or was I?

It was one of those landings that lives on in the memory for weeks afterwards and not in a particularly positive way. The lower we descended, the more unstable the plane became.

The man on the seat on the other side of the aisle looked out of the window as the lights of the airport runway came clearly into view. I overheard him whisper something to his girlfriend. "The wing flaps..." he said. Suddenly the plane began to wobble violently from side to side. This was nothing like any turbulence I had ever experienced, and with a massive roar of the engines we suddenly shot skywards. Instinctively Kate grabbed my hand in terror.

"Don't worry," I said. I wasn't worried because if I was going to die then I was going to die and I knew I could deal with it. After all, I had died many, many times before.

Eventually an announcement was made.

"The captain has decided not to land at this time. We will provide you with further information as soon as possible."

All sorts of thoughts went through my head. Was there a problem with the flaps? One of the engines? I had seen lots of flashes of light through the window. Had we been hit by lightning?

We circled the skies above Palermo in eerie silence. I don't know how many times we circled but we were going anti-clockwise and I couldn't help but feel that this was all part of the greater plan, that the energy work was already starting from high above the city. After about half an hour another announcement was made.

"We are being held in a holding pattern for now but we have plenty of fuel. We will update you as soon as we have more infor-mation."

I don't know how long we circled for but eventually we were diverted to Trapani airport, about 100 kilometres away from Palermo. Apparently there had been such a serious storm that all planes were diverted. I knew the deeper reason, that I was drawing a thread of light from above Palermo. So the light had been circled above Palermo, drawn skywards to Trapani, taken along the earth from Trapani to Palermo and right into a royal palace for that is where Kate and I were spending the night.

From Trapani we were taken by bus back to Palermo. We arrived in the city in the middle of the night. It seemed quite fitting that we arrived in the dark to the darkness. We were dropped in front of Central Station and had to walk down Via Roma and then turn left into Via Turino. Rome and Turino are the very two places in Italy that I had been involved in clearing. That was neat. Maybe Palermo was the third and final one.

We were staying in a 7th-century hotel, located in the former royal apartments of the Filangieri Palace of the Prince of Cuto. The hotel door was a massive wooden arch. A doorway had been cut into the door. Even though it was only a fraction of the size of the main door it was still very heavy as I pushed it open. Nothing could have prepared me for what I saw when I stepped over the threshold. I was in a courtyard lined with huge stone pillars. They supported a massive vaulted ceiling, again made of stone. The electric lights were yellow rather than white giving the entire courtyard an eerie and dramatic aura.

"Wow. Wait until you see this" I said to Kate as I turned to hold the door open for her. She was awed by the sight. Straight ahead was a wide, marble staircase. The hotel was on the 2nd floor and we were given room 20. As we were handed the key I noticed a massive painting of Mother Mary on the wall behind reception. Our room was painted quite a bright green and it had the feel of an old convent with the high ceilings, equally high window and a complete lack of comfort.

The hotel dining room was a lavish baroque masterpiece. As I sat eating my breakfast on the first morning, I gazed up at the exquisite mural on the ceiling. There was Medusa looking straight back at me. In fact she was everywhere in Palermo – on the packets of sugar, on posters, on paintings, on shop fronts, in shop windows and more. She was usually depicted as a head with 3 legs coming out of it. I had been told that I was on a journey of symbols and Medusa was symbolic.

"This is ridiculous," I moaned to Kate. "Medusa is everywhere but I can't read the sign. What is she trying to say to me?"

Kate had looked for the meaning of Medusa on her iPhone but hadn't found anything that I resonated with.

"Have you considered that the meaning could be allegorical?" she asked.

So I searched for 'allegory of Medusa' and the very first result was a blog written by J.R. Schaefer.

The Gods have not left, they live in the stories for us to de(S)cipher. And when you see the beauty of Medusa, you will see the road of the destined living in your own very soul. Which key do you choose? This door is unlike most doors, it is much older.

Medusa (meaning sovereign female wisdom) was the destroyer aspect of the Great Triple Goddess. In her images, her hair sometimes resembles dread locks, showing her origins in Africa. Medusa's symbol of female wisdom was her threatening, ceremonial mask. It has wide all-knowing eyes and all seeing eyes that see through us, penetrating our illusions and looking into the abyss of truth. Her mouth is deathly; it looks like a skull. It is devouring of all life, returning us to the source.

The triple Goddess, triple 3, returning us to source. Yes, that is where I was heading, back to the source, to zero point, guided in particular by the number 333. Maybe the 3 was representative of Medusa as well as Becket. Medusa is a feminine archetype who represents descent into the underworld, the subconscious. This journey into the darkness results in the acquisition of female wisdom, sometimes known as serpent wisdom. At the end of this journey we come face to face with our deepest fears.

Medusa was beheaded, and from her neck sprung Pegasus. The appearance of Pegasus in my everyday world indicated that

I had passed through the Medusa archetype and was now in touch with the protection of Pegasus. The allegory for Pegasus links to the immortality of the soul. Pegasus is said to guard the spirit when it travels into the astral plane. As a lot of the work I was doing related to the astral plane (the next level of existence from the physical world) then I was extremely thankful to Pegasus for his protection. His appearance as a protector really made sense to me.

Chapter 40

The New Pope

Palermo was Europe's grandest city in the 12th-century but in the 21st-century it was thudding with an uncomfortable undercurrent that was almost tangible. It was literally buzzing with energy. It was raw around the edges but full of hidden treasures, many of them so well concealed that we were free to wander around them undisturbed. There were Byzantine, Norman, Renaissance, Baroque and Arabic architectural gems that revealed glimpses of the former glory of this immensely interesting city.

We returned to the hotel that evening, having spent the entire day exploring the nooks and crannies of the city. As we entered the foyer we heard a woman singing. It was the receptionist. She was singing along word perfect to the church service that was taking place on the television, her hands clasped to her chest in rapture.

"New Papa," she explained, pointing to the television screen. "Sympatico Papa. He is Argentinian. Papa Argentinian," she informed us before continuing to sing.

I was surprised by 2 things. Firstly that the Pope had been elected so soon for I had somehow imagined that the decision would be made on the Ides of March. Secondly I had expected him to be a dark skinned man as Malachy's prophecy describes the final Pope as black.

The receptionist was joined by other guests as they were drawn to the TV, like witnessing the birth of a much loved and much wanted baby. I wanted to ask how they could be taken in by it all and not see through it. It's not the truth. But I didn't say anything. I stood in the midst of this somewhat surreal scene inside a 7th-century palace watching events unfolding on the television. Then Kate nudged me in the ribs.

"Look at the keys," she whispered.

"Keys?"

Sicily is the key to everything. The phrase rung in my ears like the resonance of a bell... Sicily is the key to everything.

"Yes, the keys behind reception."

On the wall behind the reception desk was a wooden cabinet with numbered compartments for the keys. Each key hung from a hook along with its enormous wooden key ring inscribed with the room number. They were moving. What was strange was that some of the keys were swinging quite violently on the hooks whilst others were perfectly still.

"Look at them swinging," said Kate.

"I can see. But why are some swinging but not others?"

"I don't know. I reckon it has something to do with what is unfolding on the telly."

I glanced at the television screen again. The adoring masses who had gathered outside the Sistine chapel to hear the news of the new Pope stood in ecstasy as the pantomime played out.

There were 9 keys on the move out of a total of 24. Tesla would have liked those numbers as they were both divisible by 3. The keys didn't stop. We stood in reception for over half an hour and there was no let up. Only much later in the evening when we went down to check our emails did we notice they had stopped. We came to the conclusion that the energy interplay between me, Kate, our location in Palermo and the unfolding events in Rome had caused an energetic disturbance that had set the keys in motion. Keys, keys, keys... "Becket," I whispered. "What do the keys mean?"

"333..." came the silent reply. 333? "Tell me more," I pleaded.

I worked out that it was 31 days since the old Pope resigned and the new one was elected. 31 is the number 13 reversed. The 112th (and last) Pope on Malachy's list was elected on March 13th, another 13. The date was 13 03 2013. Add those up and we have yet another 13. 13 is a number of great occult significance. The use of the number 13 in black magic is well documented and I'm sure that the fact that Rome has 13 obelisks is not coincidence. However, 13 is not the 333 that Becket had given me.

Of course I considered the possibility that the work that Kate and I had done in Rome was linked to the resignation of the Pope. It was almost a year since we had circled the Vatican with light on the Ides of March 2012. I went onto the site: 'http://www.time anddate.com/date/duration.html' and put in the dates of our 'Vatican webbing ceremony' and the resignation.

From and including: Thursday 15th March 2012 (the Ides of March)
To and including: Monday, 11th February 2013 (the resignation)
Result: 333 days
It is 333 days from the start date to the end date.

333 days. That couldn't be mere coincidence. To me it was clear to me that Becket had indeed been behind the work at the Vatican.

"Thank you Becket," I whispered. "Now I understand."

Chapter 41

Monreale

On March 15th Kate and I headed for Monreale Cathedral, situated on a hill high above the city of Palermo. I didn't eat the night before the Ides, just an orange and a drink of water then a very light breakfast as I prefer to be in a fasted or semi-fasted state when doing major ceremonial work. As we headed up the hill on a local bus the sky got darker and darker. The higher we climbed, the darker the sky became. By the time we reached the cathedral it was threatening rain so we were glad to get inside. We saw the mosaic representing Becket. It was in the main apse of the cathedral and it's the earliest known artistic representation of him anywhere in the world. After lighting a candle we knelt in prayer, praying for the safe manifestation of the new earth and for help and guidance in showing us the part we had to play in the unfolding new age. We thanked Becket for the guidance he had given us so far. As I knelt I reflected on the fact that it was the Ides, the central day of March. I thought about the new Pope and the fact that he had been voted in on March 13th but he was not due to be inaugurated until March 19th. I was aware that there was a six day 'gap' in the leadership of the Catholic Church and the Ides fell within this gap. How strange that I should find myself beside this famous mosaic during this unprecedented time in the Catholic Church. As I knelt there I felt Becket overshadowing me.

He let me know that his intention was to use my physical presence to slip a seed of truth into the very heart of the Catholic Church. This seed came from Becket and the effect of it would be permanently to open the doors of truth into the establishment. They could never be closed again once the seed had been planted. So I stepped through a gap in time with Becket at my side and we succeeded in placing that seed. A few moments later there was a deep rumble and the cathedral seemed to shake on its very foundations.

"What's that?" asked Kate. Before I could answer the cathedral was lit up with a brilliant flash of lightning. It cut through the high cathedral windows like a knife, illuminating the mosaic of Becket in a shocking and dramatic way.

"Christ almighty," I uttered in astonishment.

I felt the sensation in my gut as the next boom of thunder followed the first one with hardly a moment's pause. Again a blinding flash of lightning coincided with the thunder. There was a massive electric storm and it was directly overhead. Huge bolts of lightning flashed through the stained glass windows and the earth below my feet rumbled. Mythology tells us that Zeus would ride on the back of Pegasus and hurl thunderbolts. He was throwing them in our direction with wild abandon. This was a God sent clearing that I knew would deeply affect the city of Palermo. Not just Palermo but the entire area of southern Europe. This was massive. I glanced at my phone. It was exactly noon.

As I sat there my physical body began to vibrate and I could feel something happening at a cellular level. It felt like I had been hit by reflected lightning. Was it a DNA download? Then I was overwhelmed in an indescribable feeling. Not only was my body imbued with light of the highest intensity I had ever experienced, but I became as a God/Goddess. It wasn't that I was imbued with Divine energy – I WAS God, everything was God, I was everything. It wasn't an intellectual understanding, it was the actual experience of everything being God. A physical, mental and spiritual experience of Oneness.

I could have sat there all day but it was 12:30pm and the cathedral doors were closing for a long lunch, ready to reopen again at 3:30pm. We headed out into the torrential rain to catch the bus. We waited at the bus stop…and waited…and waited… For 2 hours we stood in the rain, getting soaked through to the skin because we had no umbrella. The roads were like rivers as the rainwater gushed down the hill, through Monreale and towards Palermo. The weather caused roads to close and buses to stop running. More and more rain fell and the hill on which the cathedral stood became like a gushing fountain with the water flowing down the hill towards the city of Palermo in torrents. When the bus eventually arrived and edged its way slowly back down the hill to the city below, I could see that Palermo had been washed, a cleansing in all senses of the word.

Chapter 42

Marsala

It was still raining when we arrived at the station to get the train from Palermo to Balestrate. As we left the train at the small, modern station of Balestrate I noticed a plaque on the wall.

'Se la Gioventu le neghera il consenso anche l'onnipotente e miste-riosa mafia svanira come un incube.'

This translates as :

The youth of Italy have to reject the seeming glamour and mystery of the mafia and if they do it will cease to have power.

In the town of Balestrate there was a memorial to a local policeman who had been murdered by the Mafia. Even in nonde-script places like this small resort the Mafia's presence was there and everyone was reluctant to talk about them.

After allowing ourselves a few days to settle in, Kate and I took the train from Balestrate to Marsala. Marsala translates as the port of God and we were heading there to visit the cathedral that had been dedicated to Becket. It was the Spring Equinox, March 20th. This was the new Pope's first full day in office. I told Kate about my experience in Monreale cathedral.

"It's no coincidence that we are here in Sicily during the vote for the new Pope. We are here as conduits of light that can make a difference to a billion people, the billion that have been hoodwinked by the Catholic Church."

"How so?" I asked.

"The time between old Pope stepping down and the election of the new Pope leaves a vacuum. Can you see that?"

"Yes, I can see that. A gap in between. A time when there is no Pope in office."

"It's rare. And in fact this is only the second time this has ever happened. Nature abhors a vacuum and seeks always to fill it. So it's because of the existence of this vacuum that allows us to slip in through that crack and feed truth into the ocean of Catholic consciousness. You could use the analogy of a drop of dye in a bowl of clear water. Think about how just one tiny drop of dye can tinge the entire bowl. That's what we are doing here. We have tinged the Pope void with the light of truth and have touched the consciousness of a billion people."

I loved the way that Kate used that analogy. It really helped me to understand how the seed of truth that Becket had slipped into the gap of leadership would affect the church.

"Why a billion people?" I asked.

"Because that's how many people follow the teachings of the Catholic Church. It has that many followers. Today is the first day of the new Pope and where are we heading? To a place that has a deep connection with Becket. So not only is it the Pope's first day but it's the Equinox, the day of equal day and night, a day of balance that is beyond human manipulation."

"Yes, just like the solstices which are the longest and shortest days. I find it interesting that Becket was born on the winter solstice because to me the equinoxes and the solstices are the 4 most sacred days in the annual calendar precisely, because they cannot be manipulated by man."

The train journey across inland Sicily was wonderful. We travelled through swathes of agricultural land as the train climbed steadily up quite a steep incline.

"It's good to get out into the countryside," I said as we reached a high point in the hills. "What a fantastic view."

"Yes, and look, it's 11:11," said Kate pointing to the red illuminated clock on the carriage wall. At that very moment the train braked sharply and stopped dead. We had to restrain ourselves so that we didn't fall from our seats as it was such a sudden stop.

"What the hell…?"

We looked at each other with identical expressions of open-mouthed disbelief.

"What's happened?" she asked.

I looked out of the window but there was nothing to see.

"I've no idea. But it's 11:11. There must be a reason for stopping here. Let's look for a clue."

Normally I would look for clues in advertising posters, street names, overheard conversations and so on but there was nothing at all to see, only fields of grape vines that were destined to be turned into Marsala wine. There were not even any other passengers in our carriage on this small local train.

"That's crazy. There's nothing but vines as far as the eyes can see," I said.

"Yes, not really any clue there," replied Kate.

"But you have to admit that it's really bizarre that the train has ground to a screeching halt in the back and beyond at exactly 11:11."

"Of course I agree. It's not coincidence. But what's the message?"

"Vines. Maybe it's something to do with wine?" I suggested.

"Hang on, isn't there something about vines in the bible?" asked Kate.

A butterfly flew towards the train window at that point. I interpreted that sign as hitting the truth.

"Yes there is. It's something like 'I am the vine and you are the fruit'."

"Or we're the branches. We'll have to look it up later. The message must be to do with vines because there literally is nothing else here."

We found the quote later that day. "I am the vine; you are the branches. If you remain in me and I in you, you will bear much fruit; apart from me you can do nothing." John 15:5 (a double digit and 1+5+5=11).

After a while the train began to move slowly along the single track and it crossed a bridge. Yellow-jacketed workers waved at us as we passed. I guess they were working on the rails or the structure of the bridge. That must have been why the train stopped.

The cathedral was closed when we arrived but it reopened at 3pm (of course!) and we walked through the big, heavy doors at 03:03pm. The handles of the massive doors looked familiar. They were formed of the metal letters, Alpha and Omega. I was reminded of the Alpha and Omega van in Turin. Suddenly there was a loud flapping of wings.

"Look," said Kate. "2 black birds."

"Oh, it needs to be 3 to be Becket," I replied nonchalantly. The signs had to be exact, not approximate. For example, 332, although it carries a double 3 it is not the powerful 333. Looking at the clock at 3:34 or 11:12 instead of 3:33 or 11:11 is not meaningful.

Suddenly a third bird appeared. 3 black birds, just the same as on Becket's coat of arms and we laughed. Now the sign was exact and therefore meaningful.

As I sat silently on the hard wooden bench a voice spoke in my head.

"'The Church of Rome must fall."

"What?" I asked.

"The Church of Rome must fall," repeated the voice.

"When the obelisk falls, the church will fall," it continued.

"What obelisk?"

"When the obelisk falls the Church will fall," said the voice, and I knew that this referred to the obelisk that I had leaned against over a year ago. I don't know how that could possibly happen as this obelisk has never fallen. In fact it is the only obelisk in Rome that has never fallen. I heard what was said and I registered it.

At 3.33pm we left the cathedral through alpha and omega door. Alpha and Omega, representing the first and the last, deeper than mythology, as ancient as the earth, representing the initial separation into the human experiment of duality. The Alpha and Omega was the emergence of the Fibonacci numbers and the beginning and ending of life.

I am the Alpha and the Omega, the First and the Last, the Beginning and the End.
– Revelation 22:13

Chapter 43

Glastonbury

It was April 24th 2013 and I was on my way to Glastonbury to visit Catherine. We had travelled to India together several years earlier and I had found myself in the role of carer to her as she became very ill. It was strange to find ourselves both living in the English county of Somerset. Catherine had established a retreat centre under the shadow of the famous Glastonbury Tor, the heart chakra of the world. Despite the gale force wind that was blowing that day I was intending to go up the Tor to launch my new book (*No Name No Number*) out into the world from that deeply spiritual site.

"You're not going to have a book launch up there, are you?" asked Catherine as we sat in the tranquil meditation room at her centre, sheltered from the ravages of the English spring weather.

"Yes. I'm going to do a small ceremony to bless the book before its mass release this Friday."

"You could do the ceremony here instead," she suggested. "We could put the book on the altar in the meditation room. I have some water from the Chalice Well that we could use."

Catherine is so psychic. I had not told her that I had intended using the water from the Chalice Well in the ceremony. I had decided to do that because of the fact that I was working the energy of Saint Decuman's Well. The Chalice Well is probably the most famous holy well in England. The water is rich in iron so it is slightly red. That is why it is said that the water represents the blood of Christ miraculously springing forth from the ground when Joseph of Arimathea buried or washed the cup used at the Last Supper. Like Saint Decumans well, the Chalice well was set within peaceful gardens, albeit much larger, grander and much more famous than Saint Decuman's. I quite liked the fact that the well in Watchet was not too well known and was therefore never crowded.

"And," continued Catherine, "we're right under the shadow of the Tor here so we'll be within the energy field of the earth's heart chakra."

It was true. The view from her window had an uninterrupted view of the Tor. Her place was so perfectly aligned that the doorway of Saint Michael's tower on the top of the Tor appeared in perfect profile as an open door. What's more, it just felt right. The meditation room was a powerhouse. Impressive crystals, beautiful geodes, pictures of saints and great masters, statues of gods and goddesses, talismans, Egyptian artefacts, prayer posters, flowers, plants and more filled the room.

"Okay, sounds good. Obviously I want to launch at 11:11am so we can start at 11am," I said.

So that's what we did. I placed the book upon a pair of padukas (slippers), which were laid on an orange robe on Catherine's altar. Both of these sacred objects had been blessed by Sai Baba before he died. Behind the padukas were 2 pictures of the great Yogi known as Haidakan Babaji. Catherine and I sat adjacent to each other on an armchair with our feet planted on the floor and eyes closed. There was no planning, no script, no expectation, no order. There was intention, faith and love, that's all. Neither of us had any idea what would happen. I certainly wasn't expecting a soul retrieval session to manifest...

Catherine began by reciting various invocations. Using guided visualisation we entered a space of openness and receptivity. Prayers and blessings were offered and protection was put in place. When she stated, "And restore all fragmented aspects of soul through all dimensions throughout space and time," the result was nothing short of cataclysmic. I felt a shattering of black glass throughout my auric field. This dark shattering expanded out beyond time and space. It was profound and very moving. It echoed through universes with the resonance of the Big Bang. It felt like the final battle between good and evil happening right there and then. Yet even as I observed this happening at many levels, I was conscious of that very still and serene part of me that could not be touched by any of this. The war between light and dark was not me. I was the stillness. I was the watcher.

My 5 higher chakras were activated and all vows made through all dimensions were revoked. My soul retrieval claimed back parts of me from all centuries and all dimensions. I had put my phone off and when I put it back on only one person had texted me.

SARAH 'xxx' Wednesday, 11:13.

That's all it said. 3 kisses. Sarah had texted right in the middle of the soul retrieval. That was a very odd synch because she was the person who had been responsible for the protection of the first book I had written: *The 11:11 Code.*

Sarah had been to see me a few days earlier, and had subsequently been to see another friend called Maria. The following day, Maria was in her garden when she became overwhelmed by a feeling of darkness. It seemed to engulf her and she felt her chakras close up as a form of protection. She was so concerned that she phoned her psychic friend called Edward. Edward immediately identified that Maria was under psychic attack.

"But where's it coming from?" asked Maria.

"Who have you seen recently?" asked Edward.

"Sarah."

"No, it's not her. It's coming through Sarah though."

Maria began to list the names of people either she or Sarah had seen in the previous few days. When she reached 'Hilary' he stopped her.

"Yes, it's Hilary. Who is she?"

Maria explained that I was an author who had written a book about the number 11:11, which is a spiritual code that could lead Humanity towards their true Divine purpose on earth. The book had just been printed and was due for distribution the following week.

"The dark forces do not want this book to be a catalyst for change in people," he explained to Maria. "There is a black occultist hanging around Hilary. He is trying to weave a spell on the book but he cannot penetrate Hilary's energy field because her spiritual practises give her protection. The occultist that is trying to break through Hilary's energy is looking for a way in to get to the book. His attempts to do that have affected Sarah's energy, and then yours in turn. I'll work on clearing you both then you must contact Hilary and get her to call me. It's urgent. It can't wait."

(*No Name No Number* by Hilary H. Carter)

There was no doubt in my mind that Sarah and I had a strong past life connection. I was thankful to her for enabling the protection of The 11:11 Code, and also to my Facebook friend Angela for encouraging me to perform the No Name No Number ceremony. And of course I was very grateful to have Catherine's help and support too.

After the ceremony I took the book up the Tor and offered it out to the world with love and on my return I placed it back on the padukas whilst Catherine and I had a late lunch.

"Come and look at this," called Catherine.

"What?" I asked.

"This ash. Look. It's vibhuti and it's started appearing on the padukas and the robe."

"Where has it come from?" I asked.

"It has appeared by Divine grace," replied Catherine. I was over awed at this manifestation. The appearance of vibhuti (sacred ash) is strongly linked to Sai Baba. I had seen an example of this miraculous phenomena several years earlier when I was in the town of Puttaparthi, India, the location of Sai Baba's ashram. It appeared on a picture of Sai Baba in the foyer of a hotel, growing out of the picture in the same way that moss or mould can grow on a damp wall. Now it was appearing in Catherine's meditation room. Sai Baba calls the appearance of vibhuti his 'calling card'.

"What's the date?" she asked.

"24th April."

"Hang on a minute. Are you sure?"

"Yes, I'm certain."

She rushed over to her calendar.

"I thought so!" she exclaimed. "It's the anniversary of Sai Baba's passing. It's exactly 2 years to the day that he died."

This truly was a remarkable synchronicity as neither of us had been aware of the significance of the date when we had decided to meet up. It just happened to be the first day that we were both free.

Later that afternoon I began to feel quite strange. My head hurt. It felt as if the bones in my skull were trying to re-align and I felt the need to stand on my head to try to alleviate the painful feeling. The uncomfortable sensation in my head lasted all day and I still had traces of it the following morning. I rang Catherine to tell her.

"Don't worry. It's the activation of the higher chakras causing it. It'll pass. Give it time."

She was right. It did pass. And the book *No Name No Number* was published 2 days later, birthed into the world from Glastonbury, the Isle of Avalon, the heart chakra of the world.

Chapter 44

The Wesak Moon

It was good to be tuned in to the ebb and flow of nature. From my window in Watchet I could watch the rise and fall of the tide, the second highest tidal range in the world. It came in at an alarming speed, sometimes rising by more than 11 metres in a matter of hours. I loved to walk the rugged coastline, unlike anywhere on earth I had ever been, although 'walk' might not be the most accurate term to use. There are many major fault lines at Watchet and the shoreline is very unusual. I scrambled over jagged rocks, climbed precariously over large swathes of assorted pebbles, strode over the dark grey sands and sank in the quicksand. Massive rock faces from the Triassic and Jurassic era looked as if they had just recently been heaved up from way below the earth. Apart from the region of Cappadocia in Turkey, I could not think of any landscape as strange as my local shore. Sometimes I felt as if I was on the moon. This prehistoric landscape was a geologist's and fossil hunters dream as the shoreline was littered with ammonites and the reptile remains of long extinct species. When the tide was in I took the high path above the cliffs, taking in the views across the muddy waters of the channel to the shoreline of Wales.

It was the first Wesak full moon since the ending of the Mayan calendar and I was heading up to the well to mark the occasion. The Wesak moon is the first full moon in May. It is also known as the Buddha's moon because of its link to the Buddha's birthday. The full moon was at exactly 2 minutes to 9 in the evening but I left home an hour earlier. I walked alone along the deserted public footpath just as the sun was setting. Spring was on its way. It was late that year. We had suffered an extremely harsh winter so it was wonderful to see the emerging plants. The trees were in light green bud and the grassy banks were dotted with yellow primroses. I picked some of the fresh young dandelion leaves for my salad but I would have to come back with my gloves to harvest the nettles. The path up to the well was lined with violets, an uneasy reminder of Attis and the day of blood.

Despite the late hour the paper mill was in full production, spewing out masses of white steam, adding an eerie mistiness to the already slightly misty night. I took a right turn down the tree lined stony lane and walked along in the shadow of Saint Decumans church. As I approached the gate to the well I noticed a large picture of a key on a notice at the entrance, indicating that the renovation of the well garden had been funded by 'key fund funding'. I had visited the well so many times yet this was the first time I had noticed the key.

I stepped through the gate into the sanctity of the well garden. The church tower above the lane had a slightly ominous presence, probably because it had been built from the guilt of the families of the murderous knights. There was no such feeling at the well because this had been manifested by the guilt-free Divine hand, not by human hand. The church might try and lay claim to the well but in reality it belongs to us all.

I climbed the 26 steps down to the water, being careful not to tread on the primroses that had happily spread themselves onto the steps. I prepared the well and its surroundings by clearing away some of the algae then I took some excess moss from the pipe to allow the free flow of water. A face had been scraped into the paving stone. It had one eye and looked like mythical goddess. I was alone. Where were the Pagans, the Druids and the Buddhists on this auspicious day?

I knelt by the well and dipped my finger in the crystal clear water. Suddenly the water began to behave erratically, spurting out in fits and starts as if it was reacting to the approaching full moon. Although I couldn't see it from the dip in the land where the well was, I imagined the moon bathing the entire planet in peace and by thinking this thought I was joining with others with exactly same thought form. As humans we have so much power to be able to change the world by changing our thoughts. When thousands of us hold the same thought form at the same time, we can make massive changes. There are many peacemakers on the earth right now and we are here to bring forth the age of peace. I recited the Alice Bailey invocation, ending with "Let Light and Love and Power restore the Plan on Earth". Light. Love. Power. With each of those 3 words I dipped my raw sapphire into the well.

> The beauty and the strength of this Invocation lies in its simplicity, and in its expression of certain central truths which all men, innately and normally, accept— the truth of the existence of a basic Intelligence to Whom we vaguely give the name of God; the truth that behind all outer seeming, the motivating power of the universe is Love; the truth that a great Individuality came to earth, called by Christians, the Christ, and embodied that love so that we could understand; the truth that both love and intelligence are effects of what is called the Will of God; and finally the self-evident truth that only through humanity itself can the Divine Plan work out.
> – Alice A. Bailey

As my crystal hung above the well it blended into the darkness, dissolved into the blanket of the night. Although it was suspended on a cord it began to move as if it had a life of its own. The cord felt like a rigid wooden stick. Something was going on. Some presence was taking over. And then it happened. I entered the past life that was so relevant to this present life. I was a knight kneeling over the waters of the well. I was praying fervently for the souls of Reginald Fitzurse and Le Breton, especially Fitzurse as we had a blood connection. I was doing this in the dark so that nobody could see me. It was because of a blood connection that I felt so very tainted by the knight's actions. I was begging forgiveness for all of us.

When past life recall happens the most striking thing is the depth of feeling that I experience. It's not like looking at an old photo in the family album. It's like entering the body of the person that I was and experiencing being in that body with all its physical strengths and weaknesses, the thoughts of that mind and the feelings of the emotions. In that life I was tall, strong and powerfully built. But my mind was troubled. My emotions surrounding the murder of Becket were those of guilt and tremendous shame, not just for me but for my whole family.

I had visited the well very soon after the murder. In fact I had surrendered my most precious and very valuable ring to the water as a sort of sacrifice, an offering to the Gods that I secretly believed to reside at the sacred well. As a child my auntie had taken me to the well on many occasions as she thought it was a place of sacredness, but we had to visit in secret because such pagan beliefs were frowned upon. The ring was a large, solid gold signet ring inscribed with my family crest, which I used for impressing the family seal onto letters sealed with wax.

Then I felt my 12th-century name coming through. Firstly the name 'Combe' was clearly given, followed by a name that sounded like Chaundrey. Slowly, like a blurry picture gradually coming into focus, it became clearer. De Chaundrey of Tiddecombe. The 'De' within the name clearly indicated it was of French origin... De Chauntry of Tettacombe... De Chonnsey of Ettacombe... De Chorrsey... It was coming through in old French, complete with a really heavy accent. I can best describe it like this. Imagine if you are in France in the 12th-century and you ask somebody their name. They reply with their name in a foreign language in their local dialect. If they asked you to write it down I'm sure you might struggle. That's why I'm struggling to explain how this name sounded to me. All I could do was to register the information to the best of my ability in order to research the name later on. Although I didn't realise it in that moment, matters would be taken out of my hands before I had time to begin any research.

Chapter 45

Cannington Priory

On the 111th day of the year I always take particular note of what happens and who contacts me. On 111th day of 2013 I was contacted by an American writer. Her name was Shannon Anderson and she was the author of *The Magdalene Awakening: Symbols and Synchronicity Heralding the Re-emergence of the Divine Feminine.* She had read my books about the 11:11 phenomenon and had wanted to make contact because she had been experiencing the appearance of the number 444. Because of the fact that it was 111th day I knew that it was important for me to be in contact with her so I gave her my phone number and asked her to give me a call when she was in my area.

Less than 2 weeks after the incident at the well she texted me to say that she was in England and would be passing through Somerset the following day, travelling south down the M5 motorway. She asked whether I could suggest place to meet for lunch, somewhere as near to the exit of the motorway as possible. I went online and found an interesting tearoom that I thought might appeal to her.

Hi Shannon,

I suggest meeting at Cannington, just a few miles from junction 23 of the motorway. It's a 13th-century priory near Bridgwater that has a tearoom within the walled gardens – very English! Well worth a short detour from the monotony of the motorway. Let me know if you want to meet there and if so what time would suit you. The signs around it for me are very strong. I like the 03:11:11 timing of your email…Hilary x

For some reason the email did not reach Shannon until it was too late to meet, but as I had kept the day free I decided I would go and have lunch there alone. I had never explored the area around Cannington even though it was only a few miles from Watchet. In fact it is 11 miles as the crow flies. Well, it just had to be, didn't it? The beauty of the area touched me. The gentle contours of the hills, the unspoilt rural landscapes, the fields full of buttercups, the picturesque country cottages and of course the old country churches all spoke of a bygone era. This is an area of England that few people know and appreciate. The lack of tourists was a major part of its charm.

I found the tearoom on the outskirts of the Somerset town of Bridgwater, along with a leaflet detailing its history. There was an intriguing nugget of information on the Cannington leaflet.

An inquiry in the year 1328, looked into the illicit wanderings of monks and nuns. It is said that there is a network of tunnels leading from Cannington Court to various spots in the village, which enabled the monks and nuns to meet in secret. Staff at Cannington discovered the caved-in remains of a tunnel entrance, which seems to suggest a tunnel running beneath the formal lawns in the Walled Garden. The iron bound gates to be found at the entrance to Cannington Court are said to have been erected to keep the nuns in.

My French convent had been a closed order and many local girls were admitted into holy orders by their mothers against their father's wishes. One of the elderly women in the town had told me that a tunnel out of the convent allowed these girls to escape and have 'rendez-vous' with local men, including monks. They sometimes got pregnant and the resulting babies were murdered by the older nuns. At first I had thought that was an improbable story but this leaflet helped to confirm that it could indeed be true. I continued reading the leaflet.

Located in the village of Cannington, Somerset, the Walled Gardens lie within the grounds of a medieval priory and many of its fine buildings, including the walls of the garden, remain. Cannington Priory (later Cannington Court) was first established in about 1138 by the De Courcy family – lords of nearby Stogursey.
http://www.canningtonwalledgardens.co.uk

As soon as I saw it I knew. That was my family. I was a De Courcy. Simply reading my name had a profound effect on my physical body. My heart began to thump in my chest and my knees weakened. I repeated it silently to myself. De Courcy, De Courcy... Although at first glance it doesn't appear to be the same name, if it is said with a French accent the name De Courcy is almost identical to De Chorrsey, especially if one allows for the changed pronunciation that occurs through the centuries. It said that the De Courcy family was from the village of Stogursey. Originally it had been called 'Stoke Courcy' but the pronunciation of that name too had been altered over the centuries because of the strong local dialect in Somerset. It was clear I needed to visit Stogursey and as it was only 3 miles from Cannington I called in on my way back to Watchet that same day.

The village of Stogursey was small but there was a castle. The walls of the castle were still standing and the surrounding moat was intact and still filled with water. The whole area of Stogursey (but in particular the castle) felt eerily familiar.

Although there is no known written record of the castle building until 1204, Stogursey castle was thought to have been built in the late 11th or early 12th-century. It's probable that I was in my late teens or mid 20s when the Becket stuff went down in which case I guess I must have been born around the years 1145–1150. I looked at the De Courcy family tree and found John and his brother William had both been born around that date. I am certain that I was John, the 12th-century knight known as

John de Courcy. I realise that John is a very common name. Even so, John is a very significant name in my present life as both my deceased father and my older brother carry that name, as do cousins on both sides of the family.

> Born around AD 1150, John de Courcy was a minor member of a Somerset family with important connections in the north of England. Described by the chronicler Gerald of Wales as 'fair-haired and tall with bony and sinewy limbs' and possessing 'immense bodily strength', De Courcy served Henry II in England and France before coming to Ireland in 1176. De Courcy seems to have died, perhaps in exile, in France around 1219.
> – Culture northernireland.org

That tied in with the experience at the well when I found myself kneeling within a very strong and powerful, male body. Once I had made the connection with my family name, all the memories came flooding back, that familiar feeling of a dam bursting open, lifting the lid on memories that had been suppressed for centuries because they were too difficult and painful to examine. I had known Richard le Brett and Reginald Fitzurse because we all lived in the Watchet area. I had spent time living with the Fitzurse family because we were cousins. However, I looked upon Reginald as a brother even though we may not have been brothers by blood. We were close in age and spent much of our childhood together. That's why I knew him so well and how I knew that he had always had this hot headed temper. Reginald and I both served in the court of Henry II. My grandfather was Willian II de Courcy. My father was also called William de Courcy. He was born in Williton (2 miles from Watchet) in Somerset circa 1131 in which case he would only have been about 19 when I was born, although he could have been older because, due to a lack of accurate records, none of these dates can be 100 per cent accurate. Richard le Brett was also part of my extended family network. He came from Sampford Brett (less than 3 miles from Watchet) and lived very near to the Fitzurses of Williton. He was a close friend of Henry II's brother William X so we often saw him at Henry's court. Like us Richard was French and it was him who had sliced off the top of Becket's head with his sword, breaking it as he hit him with such force.

I knew that Fitzurse had a fiery temper, but when he became fired up with the idea of killing Becket in order to gain favour with King Henry II, I did nothing to calm him down. I genuinely hadn't realised that he would actually go through with his plan to carry out the murder. So when he did kill Becket, I was filled with a sense of remorse. I kept feeling that I could somehow have prevented the murder happening. If only I had said something. If only I had diverted him. If only I had talked him out of it. If only I had calmed him down. If only, if only…

I couldn't understand why I had downloaded the name 'De Chorsey of Ettacombe' because John de Courcy was from Stoke Courcy, which didn't sound anything like Ettacombe. However, Richard le Brett's father was the baron of Odcombe and there was a place called Combwich near to Stogursey castle. There was also Hestercombe, Nettlecombe and many other local hamlets and villages with Combe in their name that I might have had a connection with. It is possible that the link with the place name Combe had been lost over time. After all, this had all happened almost a thousand years ago and in the 14th-century the plague known as the Black Death hit the county of Somerset very badly. At that time the population of some villages were totally wiped out and they fell into ruin, never to be inhabited again.

I looked for my De Courcy 12th-century family crest and it had 3 birds on it just like Becket's. There was the headpiece of a suit of armour and the Latin family motto translated as 'TRUTH CONQUERS ALL THINGS.' It seems to me as if I was still following that motto in the 21st-century.

So who had Kate been in this unfolding story? She felt as if she had observed the murder through the eyes of a monk and had said this to me on more than one occasion. In actual fact there were 4 written accounts of the murder but only one had been written by an eye witness. This was Edward Grim, a clerk from Cambridge who observed the attack from the safety of a hiding place behind the altar. He wrote his account sometime after the event. He had attempted to protect Becket, and in doing so his arm was badly wounded. Could Kate have been Grim? That question arose in my mind as I was reading his story online and suddenly an advert popped up in the corner of my laptop screen. It was advertising a hotel in Enfield, London. It said,

"Only £33:33. Instant confirmation!"

The phrase 'instant confirmation' linked to the number 3333 was instant confirmation that my gut feeling was right and Kate had indeed incarnated as Edward Grim in the 12th-century. At last I had the answers I had been seeking and I finally understood why Kate and I had been involved in this story together and why I had been led to the old house in Watchet.

Chapter 46

The New Octave

"I'm doing a talk at the town hall in Glastonbury and I have been guided to ask you to accompany me."

"Okay. I'll come along and join you."

The words were out of my mouth before I had time to run the idea past my mind. Despite the fact that it was a bit of a drive to Glastonbury, I had committed myself. I guess it just felt right.

"What's the talk about?" I asked.

"I don't know. I'm waiting for guidance on that."

Catherine lives with an incredible amount of faith. As a surrendered ego she is aware that she is an instrument of God and here to do whatever she is guided to do by the Divine hand. She was due to address a hall full of people and yet she had nothing prepared as she was intending to open herself up as a channel to be used by the Divine. Now that's what I call faith.

The next day she rang me because she was getting a download and needed to connect.

"Have you got that piece of glass that I gave you?" she asked.

"Yes, it's in my purse."

"Can you hold it while we talk?"

I placed it in my hand, a piece of blue glass inscribed with some sacred geometry. She was holding the other part. It had come from one of Catherine's healing pendants that had broken and the geometry was that of the Sri Yantra, composed of 9 interlocking triangles. On my last visit to Catherine's house she had given it to me. That same day she had taken me into a deep state of being and had facilitated the opening of my five upper chakras, the ones that were beyond the seven chakras of the body.

"I have been told that I am going to be downloading a new

frequency when I do the talk. Together as a group we are going to bringing in the Maha Anatman energy. Four of us are going to be holding the template for the new frequency: You, me and my two friends Kowtna and Jane. Jane is in Iowa but she'll connect with us beyond the physical. Kowtna is in Rejevik in Iceland. This new template is going to be anchored in Glastonbury Abbey which will be possible because the talk is taking place just outside the abbey walls."

I had never met Kowtna and Jane but that didn't matter. I trusted Catherine's channelling. Like me, she had been feeling strange for the last week or so. Even as we connected on the phone she said she felt all shaky and weak. I was aware of light charging through me. Whenever that happens, I know I am being spoken to with the voice of truth so I listen and take note. It was clear that we were being prepared for this interesting and unusual work. The next day Catherine rang again and as soon as we started talking, once more she began to channel.

"This work is pivotal. It is linked to the earth's rotation. Seven new octaves of light are being manifest. We have been prepared to hold this frequency template. A rainbow bridge will be created and the veils between the dimensions will become thinner. This has to be done in Glastonbury as this is the heart chakra of the world and the location of the first Christian church that was ever..."

She paused.

"That was ever what?" I asked.

"Just ever. The first church."

I thought the first church was in Jerusalem but I didn't want to interrupt the download so I waited for Catherine to continue.

"The town hall in which the talk will be taking place was once on abbey land. Maha means great being. That has just come through. It relates to the body of the Christos that will be anchored by the four of us. Anatman refers to no-self hence Maha Anatman. This new frequency is to be embodied by those

Christed ones with no ego-self to serve those others who are ready to embody it."

Then I had a download. Information was coming through to me via downloads more and more often. Most people who are only used to trusting information that is written down might find it difficult to trust or believe truths that are received in this way. I believe that it is because my DNA has been altered into the new DNA structure that information can be imparted in this way

'Ma and Ha are primordial sounds. They are of the right resonance to allow this new frequency through. Your Tibetan bowl is carrying those vibrations. Take it with you to harmonise the resonance of the location. This energy will come through as vibration as is all life, as is all sound.'

My Tibetan bowl had found me many years earlier when I had lived and worked with an American sound healer and gong master. Every day for months he had used his Tibetan bowls and gong to work on my energy field, bathing me in healing sound vibrations to clear my aura, unblock my chakras and shift me in consciousness. I had used my bowl for meditations when teaching yoga and I had actually seen the spirit of the bowl leap out of it on more than one occasion.

The day of the talk arrived, July 17th 2013. We pulled into the car park just beside Glastonbury Abbey. I could see the towering walls of this graceful ruin standing proudly above the stone wall of the car park.

"We need to be as near to the entrance of the town hall as possible because we've got so much to carry," said Catherine. I pulled into the very first vacant space, nose to nose with a large estate car. I couldn't help but notice the unusual number plate. It had a red and yellow motif on it. Normally English number plates are black and white. I looked more closely. I saw the letters GBM and a 3-legged symbol: the triskelion. It was an Isle of Man car. How rare. There are only about 80,000 residents on the island so the chances of an Isle of Man car being in Glastonbury and me parking next to it were incalculable.

Catherine's audience arrived. There were about 25 or 30 people of all ages, both male and female. They had no idea that they were about to play a very important role in the emergence of the new earth. Catherine put a short meditation CD on in preparation for bringing in the new octave. In this meditation we were guided to send love to Mother Earth and then wait for the love to return to us. Then we sent love to the heavens, the sky, the sun and moon and planets and waited for that love to return.

"Mother Earth is your divine mother, Father Sky is your divine father and you are the divine child. This is the Holy Trinity. You have just brought it down onto earth and made it alive," said the voice on the CD. At the mention of the Holy Trinity I was stunned.

"Find the sacred space of your heart. This is the most sacred space in the universe, the place where creation begins, the place where life begins anew."

I felt a geometric merkaba around my own body and then it connected with everybody elses until we were a single energy field. The merkaba is the energy field around the human physical body, consisting of two counter-rotating tetrahedrons, spinning with the speed of light. Through meditation, this field can be amplified.

I became aware that we were a massive, spinning column of light but not dense light. It was geometric (rather like a framework) and it extended out way beyond the town hall. It covered the entire site of the abbey. What we had actually done was to anchor in a higher octave of light. This is why the merkabas had to spin. It was a spiralling movement of energy. It spiralled in the same way that Earth spirals. Several years ago I had come to the realisation that the Earth is not a static body dangling in space. It's spiralling through space. Everything is spiralling. And so it was that on the day of Catherine's talk the Earth spiralled into a different key octave, one that resonates to the number 7 and the key C.

Catherine ended the evening with a channelling.

"There is no personal do-ership therefore no guilt. This high octave that was downloaded into your auric fields will manifest according to your destiny. Accept everything exactly as it is. No past or future. No good or bad. Just know that you walk always with enlightened beings from the levels of light who guide you every step of the way. If you no longer identify with your body and the roles that you play you will understand that you are universal consciousness. When you go to sleep at night, 'you' disappear. You awaken and the world immediately comes back. This is the world that you created. This is the play of consciousness playing its role to perfection through you. We re-affirm; there is no personal do-ership. You are One with all that is. You think you are separate from God but you have never been separate from God. 'God' can be called Universal Consciousness. It is only the ego that separates you from God. The ego is the false self, which has built up walls around the love that you truly are.

"There is no original guilt as there is no original sin. But within this play of consciousness this idea had to manifest in order for awareness to forget itself within the play. We go back to the story of the Nazarene, this great master who was one with all that is, complete awareness aware of itself, self-realised in every respect, having no dogma or creed and leaving the 'Church' into the hands of Saint Peter saying, 'On this rock I will build my church.' Down through the Ages this has been misinterpreted as man lost himself within the play of consciousness. Through this, different religions sprung up, including Christianity. Along with religion came teachings of a heavenly deity, an all-pervading power that says what is right and wrong. Therefore, guilt arose. But now, through many cycles of evolution, awareness is becoming aware of itself within this play of consciousness."

After the talk the 2 of us walked straight up to the Tor,

connecting the energy of the abbey with that of this sacred site, once known as the Isle of Avalon.

"I liked the meditation," I said as we walked back to the car.

"It was by Drunvalo Melchizadek," replied Catherine. "The flower of life guy."

"I liked the way it was about the trinity. I must look more closely at his work because that was such a synchronicity, putting on a trinity meditation when I have been experiencing such synchs around the number 33."

Having enabled the manifestation of the new octave we returned to my car. The Isle of Man car was still parked opposite mine. It was then that I noticed the model of the car. It was a Skoda *Octavia*, confirming that the *Octave* work had been successful.

Chapter 47

Drunvalo

Drunvalo Melchizedek wasn't born into a physical body and named as Drunvalo Melchizedek at birth. He was a walk-in. A 'walk-in' is when an advanced being takes over the body of someone already in human form through a prearranged agreement with that soul. This is not to be confused with possession, which is when a disincarnate spirit takes over a person without their permission. I have witnessed that with my own eyes and it was not a pleasant experience. Catherine had experienced a walk in herself some years ago when she had almost left her body in death. That's how she was able to access the knowledge and information that she channelled.

I soon discovered that just about everything I had encountered on my journey with numbers and signs seemed to be connected to Drunvalo. For example, he had studied at the Alpha and Omega Order of Melchizedek in Vancouver, Canada. The Melchizedek consciousness is the direct connection and source to God. All of the Melchizedeks on Earth (Drunvalo is not the only one) work through the Alpha and Omega Order.

Drunvalo Melchizedek says that through meditation the human being is able to access and receive guidance from high sources of awareness. That is exactly what happened to me. After decades of practising yoga and meditation I started receiving guidance from high sources that I refer to as my Higher Self. For me personally, the guidance came through numbers. To be aware enough to notice the number signs I need to be in the moment and fully observant of my perceived world. This in itself is a state of meditation. Meditation doesn't necessarily mean sitting still with the spine erect and the eyes closed. What meditation does is to train the mind to be still and to be able to focus your attention on the present moment. It is quite possible to be in a meditative state as you go about your daily life with full awareness.

Drunvalo's explanation of the trinity is that it is beyond religion and it guides us to the real source of truth within the sacred space of the heart. The triskelion on the flag of Sicily is a visual representation of the trinity and Medusa herself is a part of a trinity, one of 3 sisters known as the Gorgons. The archetypal energy of Medusa had put me in touch with my deepest fear. For me, that was the fear that I had somehow failed to prevent the murder of the great saint, Thomas Becket.

Cybele, like the Black Madonna, is part of the Divine Feminine that has been suppressed for many centuries. The Church has presented feminine energy in the form of Mother Mary, the virgin, the pure and gentle. The male dominated Church suppressed the powerful, creative, wise side of the Divine Feminine as they feared it. Because of the link with Cybele and castration I can quite understand why men might be afraid but the suppression caused an imbalance. The dark feminine devours. She destroys the status quo. This is a necessary part of creation because, within the world of duality there has to be destruction in order for there to be creation. Now the dark aspect of the Divine Feminine is re-emerging and balance is being restored.

The Black Madonna brings up our dregs, our hidden stuff, our shadow. It is through this process that we can come back to balance on an individual level. I had thought that I was working with Divine Feminine energy over the past few years but in fact I had been working specifically with the Black Madonna. From the moment that she came eye to eye with me on the balcony of my Spanish convent she has been with me. As I walked into places of darkness in my role as a light worker, I was walking into the congealed mass subconscious of humanity. I walked without fear, allowing the light of love to shine into those pockets of stagnation, thereby releasing blocks at the physical and astral levels of existence, in preparation for the new earth that is being born.

The trinity (and therefore the number 3) also represents the triple goddess and the creator/destroyer/preserver. Duality (and thereby the number 2) cannot exist without the number 3 being involved. That's because of the relationship between the 2 opposing forces of duality: for example, hot/cold/warm, high/low/middle, right/left/centre, creator/destroyer/preserver and so on.

The symbol of the triskelion is thought to come from the time of Atlantis, that mysterious lost continent that many believe lies hidden under the Atlantic Ocean. The triskelion is also known as the spiral of life. The three spirals are interconnected and each spiral turns in the same direction. They represent balance, harmony and continual motion.

Drunvalo states that if you live from your heart it sets up a vibration that can be recognised by the earth. In the sacred space of the heart we have recorded everything that we have ever experienced. I realised then that the heart cases in the museum *were* the keys that I had been looking for. The heart cases were located in the city of Taunton on the famous Michael/Mary ley line, sitting right next to the reliquary from Woodspring priory. I could see the perfection of Becket's and the 2 heart cases sitting together in the display case in the museum of Somerset. I also understood why I had been guided back to the life as a woodcutter during my Quantum Healing Hypnosis because in that particular life my heart had been broken so deeply that I lost faith in God. I needed to forgive the energy that I referred to as God in order to move on and to be able to access that space in my own heart. To be in your heart and to live life from this space requires giving up the ego. You can't be living fully from your heart and still have ego. It simply isn't possible. It's a contradiction. I believe that numbers can lead you to the space in the heart.

I understood that the appearance of Medusa, Pegasus and other mythological figures had appeared to guide me back to the original stories and the original thoughts that had created the universe. Their appearance as archetypes had led me to a deeper understanding of how mythological beings can speak to us directly, beyond the restrictions of time and space.

Drunvalo's take on human history resonated with me. For the first time in my life I found myself reading an account of human history that made sense. He states that Joseph of Aramathea was Jesus's uncle and that he brought Jesus to the Isle of Avalon at the age of 12 to study in the Druid school. The Druids (like the Essenes and the Coptics) had come out of Egypt and had established a school on Glastonbury Tor. They gave land to the early Christians and the first church was built at the foot of the Tor. This was on the site where the ruins of Glastonbury Abbey still stand. 2 springs of red and white water flow through the abbey and it was from these mingled waters that the first baptisms took place. This tied in with what Val had channelled regarding 'the first church ever'.

In this third dimension we are immersed in the duality of opposing forces. However, when viewed from the 4th dimension all this 'good and bad' stuff can be seen as different aspects of the One Creator working in harmony. As Catherine put it in one of her channellings:

'Light and dark are necessary because we are in duality. Those that appear to be dark can be lighter than light beings. Some of them are higher souls because they clothed themselves in darkness in order to take the light beings into their places for the ascension so there should be no judgement because all are playing their parts exactly as was written in the play of consciousness. Wake up now. Wake up from the dream. It's all over. Step into your power. You are God realised. You had just forgotten it.'

Duality can't play out without darkness. It needs darkness

and light and all oppositions. I had heard it said that the path of darkness (known as the left hand path) has the same destination as the right hand path, which is the path of light. Even the number 333 has its dark side as it is the number of the demoness Choronzon. That is why it is very important on the path of number to run everything past your intuition before acting. I used to always ask, "Does this feel right?" before I acted on a sign. Now I don't even need to ask that question because my default setting is intuition. I find it helps to have a strong personal practise of yoga, meditation or prayer. The dark forces hate order and discipline because they thrive on chaos. My connection to the Divine energy has always protected me when I have ventured into deep, dark places where angels might fear to tread. Prayers of protection are ingrained into my memory banks ready to be used whenever I feel in need of assistance.

Now that we are evolving beyond duality we are returning to the pure light of consciousness but now we are carrying the knowledge of good and evil. We also carry all the memories and experiences that we encountered whilst living in duality. For me, although I had spent many lives in religious institutions and had been a Troubadour, Templar and Cathar in France many lives ago, I had also explored the darker side of human existence.

At last I understood yin/yang symbol. Within duality nothing is 100 per cent light or 100 per cent dark. There is duality within the duality. I believe that is why the number 11 appears as 11:11. It is positive male/negative female – negative male/positive female. The further into duality humanity went, the further away from zero point we went therefore the further from the central numbers of the Fibonacci series. You could compare it to having an eye test. When your vision is minus 8 then everything is a blur. As the lens power is increased, the world starts to come into focus. The nearer to 20:20 vision you get, the clearer the images. So if we're deep into the illusion of ego then we can't see clearly. At that stage we believe the physical world to be the true reality.

Once we begin to see through the world of illusion and start working towards releasing the ego, the world of number can be seen more clearly. I'm talking literally here. When we get to the 3 2 1 1 0 0 1 1 2 3 at the centre of the reflected Fibonacci series and these numbers start appearing in our everyday life, we can at last see our destination in sight. Everything comes into focus and our destination becomes clear, namely the return to Oneness. We are not separate from each other and each of us is a unique and equally valuable divine being. How do we get these numbers to appear in our life? With intention, as mentioned earlier in Solomon's secret 3:

"Human beings evolve and with intent can accelerate the evolutionary process."

I had spent years searching for the answer to 'Why does the 11:11 appear in my life?' and finally I had an answer. My practical research had not been in vain. All the difficulties and challenges I had encountered had borne fruit and during the process of searching for the answer I had transformed into a completely different person. What a journey it had been.

My 333 journey had led me to forgive myself for the part I thought I had played in Becket's murder. I had judged myself as guilty of failing to prevent the murder. But without judgement, there can be no guilt. And without duality how can there be judgement? Once we have dealt with any guilt that we are carrying, whether it is from today, last week, last year or from a previous life, then we are freed. I recalled my dream of a small child holding a tablet that held details of all lives ever lived and now I understood the message of the dream. The number 33 had taken me to Watchet to release me from the last shackles of guilt that I had been carrying in my energy bodies from my time as a 12th-century knight. I sometimes wonder if I would have been able to heal it if I had not chosen to follow the path of number but as soon as that though arose I observed it as a 'what-if' thought and I let it go. Now, thanks to the guidance from numbers, I was finally free of the guilt that I carried from my association with Becket's murderers.

www.drunvalo.org

Chapter 48

The Watcher of Watchet

I felt a deep sense of fulfilment after discovering why the number 333 had led me to Watchet. As is often the case on the path of number, the early days had been difficult, but as always there is a higher reason for being in the places I am led to. I am led to my personal healing at the deepest levels whilst at the same time I heal Mother Earth. It's a 2 way process.

The single eye that had appeared during the 333 journey is linked to the third eye and the pineal gland. The 4th dimension is not somewhere else. It's right here on earth but it's a state of consciousness that opens to you as your pineal gland opens. It gives heightened awareness and expanded vision. This is what allows me to access higher knowledge and to see and hear beyond the physical universe. Everything external we perceive is the externalisation of our consciousness summarised in the phrase 'as within so without', so the eye appearing was indicative of my third eye beginning to open.

My understanding is that the numbers 23 and 32 appear in your world to indicate the breakdown of your conditioning. You could say that your brain's hard drive is being wiped. Then the 11:11 appears to guide you onto your spiritual path. This is followed by the symbol of the eye as you approach zero point which represents the watcher and the watched merging into One. At this point you have broken through the doorway of consciousness that separates the third and the fourth dimensions. This is the most difficult part to break through but once you are in the fourth dimension the doorways to other dimensions open up to you much more easily.

Once I had uncovered and released my past life connection to Watchet, my life began to settle down. Gradually the house was improved. The landlord put in new windows on the top floor. In doing so the original, solid walls were exposed and I could see that the house had been built with rubble from the nearby beach. The cracks in the outside render were filled and the outside was decorated from top to bottom. The leaking windows on the ground and first floor were repaired as were the leaking gutters. I bought new carpets and curtains and put colourful flowerpots outside the front door. With regular use of dehumidifiers and damp traps along with the liberal use of essential oils, the house gradually lost its awful smell. The neighbour informed me that our row of 3 houses had been built in 1825. What's more, mine had once been the reading room for the town of Watchet. Before the war, in the early years of the 20th-century the house had been filled with books. It was a place where the people of the town could come and read books and newspapers. They couldn't be taken away like a library. The reading had to take place within the walls, so once again I found myself living in a place of education. This was the pattern of my life. In the previous 10 years I had lived in a former school of illustrious studies in Spain (16th-century), a teaching convent in France (probably 11th-century) and a former convent school in Clevedon, England. I had been guided to all of these places by numbers.

I have become very fond of the charming little town of Watchet with its deep history and quirky character. My personal memories of 1000 years ago have been released into the light of awareness and I am no longer weighed down by those medieval shackles of guilt. As I write these words I can hear Fred Bacon the local poet playing his Scottish bagpipes as he marches along the harbour wall. 90-year-old Jack Binding is doing his shift as a volunteer at the museum underneath the Holy Cross Chapel. The local artists are working in their studios overlooking the water. The dredger is busy in the harbour trying to deal with the mud, sucking it up and throwing it out to sea only for it to be swept back in on each incoming tide. The volunteers at Watchet railway station (it's on the route of the longest Steam heritage Railway in the UK) are busy at work welcoming tourists to the town. The first steam train of the day to head south is hooting as it heads towards Blue Anchor beach. I glance down at the time on my laptop. As usual it's on time. It leaves every day at exactly 11:11am (really!).

As much as I enjoy living in this characterful town, I am not complacent. I know that if the number signs appeared and guided me away from Watchet then I would follow them. I have learned not to be too attached to any particular place. I am like the flotsam on the tide going wherever the tides take it. I am human flotsam and my 'tide' is the number signs. I totally trust that the signs will lead me to where I am needed for my own highest good and for the highest good of others. I could be in Watchet for the rest of this earthly life or I could be gone next week. It makes no difference to me.

I spend a lot of time observing the harbour, watching the yachts enter and leave on the tide. Because the harbour is tidal the boats have to wait in the channel until the tide allows them to enter. Nothing can be done to hurry this process. The tides can be predicted with a high degree of accuracy and their control is beyond the hands of man. There is another tide and that is the tide of ascension. It has started coming in. We are on our way to the 4th and 5th dimensions and some humans are there already. Just like the rising waters of the Bristol Channel, nothing can stop this tide coming in. What an exciting time to be alive!

AXIS MUNDI
BOOKS

Axis Mundi Books provide the most revealing and coherent explorations and investigations of the world of hidden or forbidden knowledge. Take a fascinating journey into the realm of Esoteric Mysteries, Magic, Mysticism, Angels, Cosmology, Alchemy, Gnosticism, Theosophy, Kabbalah, Secret Societies and Religions, Symbolism, Quantum Theory, Apocalyptic Mythology, Holy Grail and Alternative Views of Mainstream Religion.